CW00547256

Faking It

Best wishes

Mandy

Faking It

Published by The Conrad Press Limited in the United Kingdom 2022

Tel: +44(0)1227 472 874
www.theconradpress.com
info@theconradpress.com

ISBN 978-1-914913-91-4

Typesetting and Cover Design by:
Charlotte Mouncey, www.bookstyle.co.uk

The Conrad Press logo was designed by Maria Priestley.

Printed and bound in Great Britain by Clays Ltd, Elcograf S.p.A.

Faking It

from bookie's son to baron:
the incredible life of Brian Leese

Mandy Moore

For my daughters Abigail, Emma and Kirsty

Acknowledgements

I amassed a great deal of photographic and documentary evidence to produce this book, some of which came from family archives and research but much of which has been with the help of others. I would especially like to thank my husband, Reg Race, who supported me and provided invaluable additional research and editing.

My sources have included Professor Martin Stannard's biography of Muriel Spark which provided many insights into Brian de Breffny's life in Rome and Susana Walton's biography of her husband - the composer William Walton -which mentioned their friendship with Brian. Also, I could not have done it without access to so much background information, documentary evidence and newspaper archive material on the internet.

My thanks go to the National Library of Scotland, the National Library of Ireland and Books Ireland, for their help in trying to track down photographs of the pre-digital era, and to give me, where appropriate, authority to use what could be retrieved. I am also grateful to the individual photographers who gave me permission to use their work, especially those who gave permission gratis.

I would like to thank the people who produced this book: James Essinger, my publisher; Erica Martin who sourced and accessed many photographs for me; and Charlotte Mouncey who edited the pictures and supervised typesetting.

I hope that any surviving relatives of Brian's who read this do not find it upsetting if they did not know his story, but I have tried to provide evidence for all that I have written and I believe, as a relative of his myself, the correct and unvarnished true story of Brian's life was one that needed to be told.

Mandy Moore July 2022

Contents

Picture and documents credits

1. Gun Street 1890 (Courtesy of Tower Hamlets Local History Library and Archives, London Borough of Tower Hamlets)
2. Dorset Street 1902 (NMUIM / Alamy Stock Photo)
3. Gravel Lane 1910 (photographer Charles Goss 1864-1946)
4. Trafalgar School, Twickenham c.1910 (author's family archive)
5. Brian's parents and grandparents holidaying in Margate c.1930 (author's family archive)
6. Moses and family on the prom in Margate c.1930 (author's family archive)
7. Myer Leese and Brian's cousin Joyce Lees c.1932 (author's family archive)
8. Brian's grandparents Myer and Rebecca Leese c.1932 (author's family archive)
9. Brian's uncle Joe and cousins on holiday in Southend c.1930 (author's family archive)
10. RMS Queen Elizabeth steaming into New York c.1949 (By courtesy of The University of Liverpool Library, Cunard Archive (Stewart Bale): D42/PR1/22/9 (2))
11. Marguerite Leese demonstrating hat-making in Deseret News 1950 (photographer unknown)
12. ZCMI Building, Salt Lake City c.1950s (Used by permission, Utah State Historical Society)
13. Mormon Temple, Salt Lake City c.1950s (Used by permission, Utah State Historical Society)
14. Guy Strutt with his father 1938 (archive PL / Alamy stock photo)

15. The Waltons c.1955 (©John Deakin / John Deakin Archive / Bridgeman Images)
16. Brian de Breffny and Princess Jyotsna's marriage certificate 1960 (© Crown Copyright)
17. Princess Jyotsna's father and grandfather at the Ranelagh Polo Club 1928 (TopFoto)
18. View of Aldenham House through the gates (PH/M/22/92 Shropshire Archives)
19. Princess Jyotsna leaving the Divorce Court 1968 (ANL/ Shutterstock)
20. Sophia Loren in Via Frattina, Rome 1963 (© Keystone Pictures USA/ZUMAPRESS.com/Mary Evans)
21. Muriel Spark 1965 (Science History Images / Alamy Stock Photo)
22. Queen Frederica of Greece 1969 (Evening Standard/Hulton Archive/Getty Images)
23. Brian in Italy c.1960 (photographer poss. George Mott)
24. 'The Irish World' book launch 1976 (with many thanks to Books Ireland, Wordwell Ltd for permission to use this photo)
25. The British Colonial Hotel, Bahamas 1950s (Mary Evans / Grenville Collins Postcard Collection)
26. Stafford Sands and Hjalmar Schacht 1962 (Bundesarchiv, Bilt183-B1107-0043-016/Hjalmar Schacht)
27. Otto Skorzeny 1943 (Sueddeutsche Zeitung Photo / Alamy Stock Photo)
28. Meyer Lansky 1970 (Granger, NYC / TopFoto)
29. Sir Stafford Sands and Lady Ulli Sands 1966 (with many thanks to the family of the late Roland Rose the photographer for permission to use this photo)
30. Stafford Sands on the Bahamian banknote (Adriana Lacob/ Shutterstock)
31. Villa Corner della Regina (ReallyEasyStar/Maurizio Sartoretto/ Alamy Stock photo)
32. Ulli and Brian de Breffny 1980s (Image Courtesy of the National Library of Ireland)
33. Castletown Cox exterior 1983 (© photographer Derry Moore)
34. Castletown Cox grand entrance hall 1983 (© photographer Derry Moore)

35. Castletown Cox drawing room 1983 (© photographer Derry Moore)
36. Castletown Cox view through doorway 1983 (© photographer Derry Moore)
37. Birr Castle still from Stately Meals programme 1981 (RTE Archives)
38. Birr Castle still from Stately Meals programme 1981 (RTE Archives)
39. Birr Castle still from Stately Meals programme 1981 (RTE Archives)
40. Viscount de Vesci and Sita de Breffny's marriage 1987 (Irish independent 7th September 1987. IND 987-171 /Image Courtesy of the National Library of Ireland.)
41. Abbeyleix House (AA World Travel Library / Alamy stock photo)
42. Viscount and Viscountess de Vesci at Ascot (ANL/Shutterstock)
43. Ulli de Breffny c.1988 (Image Courtesy of the National Library of Ireland)
44. Marguerite Leese death certificate 1980 (© Crown Copyright)
45. Moses Leese death Certificate 1981 (© Crown Copyright)
46. Brian de Breffny gravestone 2021 (with many thanks to Michael Gaul for permission to use this photograph)

Preface

*'He is not a man given to reminiscing about the past.
I know next to nothing about his earlier years'.*

Sita Maria de Breffny, Brian's daughter.

Researching Brian's life was like following a trail of breadcrumbs, as one incredible fact led to another and another. It was nothing less than a trail of deception, perjury and lies.

Tracing family history is like detective work; much of it is mundane, but then you come across a person like my mother's cousin Brian Michael Leese, an astonishing character who reinvented himself time and again. He changed his name and what he called himself on numerous occasions, and by doing so climbed the greasy social pole to emerge as an Irish baron.

As I looked into my mother's family, Brian's life began to unfold before me and I could hardly believe it. I started to dig deeper and the twists and turns were so bizarre I knew that of all the stories in my family's past, this was the one that needed to be told.

Here was a man who had started out as an ordinary boy from London who had reinvented himself as an Irish baron – and he was my first cousin once removed. He, like me, researched his family history, but he used his skills as a genealogist to look for ways to advance his own image and interests, and it led to him distancing himself from his parents and transforming himself completely.

What turned Brian, the son of a Jewish bookie-cum-taxi driver and a woman of Irish heritage living in Twickenham, into the fantasist calling himself Baron de Breffny who married an Indian princess, then a Finnish multi-million heiress, mixed with celebrities and royalty, led an extraordinarily privileged life, and whose daughter married into the top echelons of the British aristocracy?

We will never know the full answer to that critical question, but as Brian progressed through his life, the stories he told about his origins, education and ancestry meant that one falsehood inexorably led to another and he appears on many occasions to have forgotten what the original story was, so contradictions and complications became apparent to even the casual observer. In later life he just brazened this out, shrugging off questions as impertinence, but the truth cannot remain hidden forever.

Brian may have ended up thinking of himself as a baron but that wasn't where he started out. This is the intriguing story of who Brian really was, the unvarnished truth about the bizarre journey he took from his humble origins in London via the Mormons in Salt Lake City, celebrity parties and bisexual affairs in Ischia and Rome, and a Palladian mansion in Ireland, to become an author, an authority on Irish architecture and the darling of Irish high society, all the while pretending he was a highly educated intellectual who had studied at multiple universities to buttress his claim to be an Irish baron. He even lied about where he was born and who his parents really were.

His story is tangled up with organised crime on the racecourses of England, corruption and Nazis in the Bahamas, the mob in America, world renowned composers and authors and ended up with him living off the proceeds of Mafia money.

I have to admire his 'chutzpah', his determination to succeed, the desperate desire to be someone in a world of nobodies. For better or for worse, this is his story.

1. Two lucky escapes – out of Amsterdam and the East End

When Brian stepped onto the Queen Elizabeth in Southampton on his way to America, little did he know how much that journey would change his life; but his story starts long before he set sail. It could be said to begin with another journey, that of his great grandfather, Moses Meijer Leist, who left Amsterdam for East London in the 1860s – a move that was to secure the future of many generations of his family and save them from the holocaust.

At the time of the 1853 Dutch census, when Moses Meijer Leist was just ten years old, the family was living at 220 Houtstraat, Korte, in Amsterdam. When he moved to London just a few years later, he left behind nine brothers and sisters, although only five of his siblings - his sisters Betje, Vrouwtje, Schoontje, Klaartje and Esther - survived into adulthood.

His sisters married and had children, but most of these children and their families were shipped from Amsterdam to Auschwitz, Sobibor and other of Hitler's death camps across Europe. All were murdered in that horrendous episode in history; so by leaving Amsterdam and travelling to London, Moses Leist ensured that Brian was born.

In the nineteenth century many Dutch Jews decided to move to London, even though Jews in Amsterdam were not as badly off as those in other European countries. The East End of London was a major producer of cigars and many working in that industry found the conditions in London far more acceptable than in Amsterdam.

Numerous workshops were situated in Bethnal Green, Whitechapel and Spitalfields, all close to the Tobacco Dock in Wapping where the leaf tobacco would come in from the United States, to be processed into cigars and cigarettes.[1] Moses Leist lived in Fashion Street, Spitalfields in 1865 when he married Hannah Dickie at the Great Synagogue Chambers, Duke's Place[2] and both Moses, now calling himself Morris, and his father-in-law worked as cigar makers.

East End squalor

Whitechapel and particularly the streets around Spitalfields Market became a melting pot, bringing together displaced Sephardi and Ashkenazi Jews from around the world. In 1899 there were whole areas where the population was almost 100 percent Jewish.[3] Poverty, overcrowding, illiteracy[4] and disease were rife; houses were rundown, without piped water or sanitation, and were rat infested; more than half the children born there died before they were five years old, and many women and children turned to prostitution as the only way to survive.

Crime abounded with pickpocketing, drunkenness and burglary commonplace. This was the hunting ground of Jack the Ripper: Millers Court off Dorset Street, Hanbury Street, and Thrawl Street were all places where the Ripper's victims died, close to Spitalfields where Moses and his family lived.

Brian's grandfather, Myer Lees (the spelling of the family surname changed several times),[5] was born on 4 February 1874 at 29 Gun Street,[6] a road leading up to Spitalfields Market. Number 29 was a general shop; in 1881 it housed seven people in the shop itself with a further fifteen living above it, including Moses, Hannah and four of their six children, one of whom was Myer.[7] Both Moses and later Myer were hawkers selling fruit in and around Spitalfields.

Brian's grandparents, Myer Leese and Rebecca Joseph were married in the East London Synagogue, Mile End[8] on 31 August 1892. At the time they were living with Rebecca's parents at 5 South Block Buildings, Stoney Lane, Houndsditch. Rebecca's mother, Esther Mendoza came from a Sephardi family whose antecedents lived in Seville, Spain before arriving in London via Amsterdam. Her father Jacob Joseph was Ashkenazi.

By 1899 Myer and Rebecca had moved out of number 5 and were living at 14 South Block.[9] South Block was one of several artisans' dwellings built in the 1880s by the Commissioners of City Sewers, to try to alleviate the overcrowding and poverty of the area, with the Block later maintained by the City of London Corporation.[10] However, these tenements, although relatively new, were still too small to accommodate the number of children many families had, at a time when birth control was either unknown or primitive, and multiple tenants had to share a bathroom and toilet.

Because of overcrowding, children were often farmed out to aunts and uncles or grandparents, as was the case with Myer and Rebecca. In 1901 three of their younger children lived with them at 14 South Block:[11] Esther, Kate and Moses (Brian's father). Moses was born there in 1900,[12] as were his younger brothers Joseph and Henry in 1902 and 1903, respectively. Hannah Lease, Myer and Rebecca's oldest child, was living with Rebecca's parents at number 5.

Esther and Moses both went to Gravel Lane School, just off Petticoat Lane.[13] Stoney Lane and Gravel Lane have now been completely demolished and replaced with modern office blocks and bars.

Follow the money - A move to Twickenham

In the early 1900s the family moved from the squalor of London's East End, where they lived in an artisan's block sharing bathroom and toilet facilities with multiple tenants, to a house in the leafy suburbs of Twickenham,[14] where Myer and Rebecca's eighth child, Dorothy, was born.

Moses was 'removed' from school in the East End on 22nd September

1905[15] and this is probably when the move took place. Moses may then have gone to the newly built Trafalgar Infants School in Elmsleigh Road close to the family's first home in Heath Road, Twickenham.[16] His younger brother Henry (my grandfather) was certainly there as we have a school photograph of him from the time.

The Leese family had escaped from the poverty and squalor of the East End into much more salubrious surroundings. A move that must have taken considerable resources.

The family story told by Brian's cousin - my mother Joyce Lees[17] - was that Myer won or made some money 'on the horses', which made this move possible. Exactly where the money came from and how much we will never know, but Myer may well have got himself involved in illegal gambling in the East End to acquire the funds, as in 1903 he was working as a labourer,[18] but after the move to Twickenham he became a commission agent – a euphemism for an off-course bookmaker[19] – and by 1921 Myer (who was now known as Mickey Lees) and then his sons Moses (known as Mickey Lees Jnr) and Joseph, became Bookmakers.[20] His youngest son Henry worked in a bookmakers run by Thomas Henry Dey[21] in Bond Street[22] so the family was heavily involved in the betting industry and therefore money derived from 'the horses' is the most likely explanation of their happier financial status.

The dangerous world of bookmaking

After the First World War racecourses became increasingly popular as the only place where legalised gambling could take place and because of this, vast amounts of money were generated. It was an unregulated business which meant that anyone could set themselves up as a bookie and the amount of money carried around on racecourses attracted the attention of criminal gangs.

Early in the twentieth century one of Birmingham's gangs, the Brummagem Boys led by the former 'Peaky Blinder' Billy Kimber, spread their network to the lucrative streets of London, and when they met resistance they would turn racetracks into battle grounds.[23] London already had numerous gangs controlling the racetracks but many of these were swept aside.

Protection rackets were rife with bookies having to pay to stand at their pitches, and one of the main income streams for Darby Sabini, an Italian gangster known as 'king of the racecourse gangs', and his Clerkenwell based organisation, was money raised by a protection racket in which Jewish bookmakers paid handsomely to be shielded from other crooks, get the chalk and other equipment they needed and to be allowed to ply their trade.

Confrontation with the vicious Brummagem Boys was inevitable; the Jewish gangster Alfred Solomon made an enemy of Billy Kimber and the Italian Darby Sabini and another Jewish gangster Edward Emanuel were also involved in the violence. Following these incidents, a number of the Brummagems were imprisoned, and the Sabinis increased their control of the racetracks. How Myer and his sons fitted into this nest of criminal activity is impossible to say. But what is clear is who my grandfather, Henry Lees, and his father Myer, worked for.

In the 1920s my grandfather was working as a clerk for the book-maker Thomas Dey, who had employed Billy Kimber as a minder to protect him from the gangs.[24] Myer was working as a Tic-tac man[25] - a bookmaker at a racecourse who took bets and communicated informa-tion about betting odds to other bookmakers using special hand and arm signals. He worked for Walter Beresford[26] who, back in 1902, had been convicted for running an illegal gaming house and, as a commis-sion agent, had also been convicted of unlawfully running a house for betting on horses; both convictions carried enormous fines.[27]

Beresford became a wealthy man from these activities and went on to become a legitimate on-course bookmaker. In 1921 he became the first President of the Racecourse Bookmakers and Backers Protection Association, which was formed to give some protection to the exposed bookies at racecourses and mitigate the violence and robbery that was rife.

Neither the racing authorities nor the police could provide adequate protection however, so the Association turned to the Sabini gang to provide it. One of the Association's salaried stewards was Darby Sabini himself and its Vice President was another noted East End criminal Edward Emanuel known as 'the Jewish Al Capone'.

When some of the Brummagems were released from prison the race-tracks descended into violence once again, with a bitter and violent racecourse war breaking out between them, and a powerful combination of the Anglo-Italian Sabinis and their Jewish supporters from Whitechapel. During 1922 there were a series of razor attacks and slashings. Then the shootings started.[28] This gang warfare lasted well into the 1930s and was the day-to-day environment in which Myer and his sons, including Brian's father, worked.

2. The Leese family in the thirties

Myer and Rebecca Leese worked their way up the property ladder in Twickenham ending up in a large house in Amyand Park Road and Myer, now known as Mickey Lees,[29] was listed in the 1922 phone book.[30] For a family to have made the move from the East End to Twickenham, move houses, and have a telephone at this time is very unusual and shows what a huge change in their financial circumstances there had been.

Moses and Marguerite, Brian's parents, married on 13th August 1923 at the Fulham Register Office in the presence of the bride's parents, Charles and Sarah O'Dell.[31] Marguerite, known in the family as Daisy, was born[32] and grew up in Fulham, West London;[33] the family lived in Gilstead Road and Daisy went to Langford School[34] in the same road.

Marguerite's family was of Irish heritage (a fact Brian later relied on to help him reinvent himself as an 'Irish baron'). Her family, the O'Dells, lived in the Sands End area of Fulham where her father was a tile fixer, and although she and Moses were married in Fulham they went to live firstly in Gordon Avenue, where Marguerite's brother Francis also lived with them,[35] and then St Margaret's Road, Twickenham.[36]

When Brian, an only child,[37] was born on 14 January 1931 at 66 Gordon Avenue, Twickenham, his parents were living close to his grand-parent's family home in Amyand Park Road. At the time of Moses and Marguerite's Marriage, Moses had been a bookmaker like his father, but by the time of Brian's birth he had become a taxi driver.[38] By 1934 the family had moved to a larger house in St Margaret's Road, Twickenham, and Marguerite's father Charles was living with them.[39] Marguerite's mother had died in 1927 and her father died 8 years later in 1935. In the 1930s, Moses' and most of his siblings all lived within walking distance of each other and some even in the same roads.[40]

When Brian was a young child he would have had several of his cousins living close by: Joe and Renee Lees, his uncle Joe's children; my mother Joyce Lees, his uncle Henry's child; and Pamela Hayward, his aunt Esther's child.[41]

Marguerite obviously doted on Brian. When he was five she organised a lavish birthday party for him and it is highly likely that his cousins would have been among the guests. In later life Brian told the story of this party and the 'beautiful golden chairs' Marguerite had rented for it. Brian obviously had no choice in who was invited to the party; he told his mother that if a girl he hated was coming then he wouldn't come himself; his mother called his bluff and made him sit the party out while all the other children enjoyed themselves.[42]

Although the 1930s was a time of global economic depression and political crisis, the Leese families were not amongst those most affected. They enjoyed punting on the River Thames at Richmond and took numerous holidays together in Margate and Southend. My mother knew Brian's parents as Uncle Mick and Aunt Daisy, but in all the holiday snaps and family pictures she had of her Jewish grandparents, aunts, uncles and cousins, there are none of Brian himself - only the children of his father's brother Joe and sisters Esther and Dorothy.

Moses' father Myer died in February 1936 and was at the time a 'Racecourse Representative', involved in the racing world until the end. He left just over £436 in his will, the equivalent of about £32,000 today. His wife Rebecca stayed on in the house in Amyand Park Road and her daughter Nancy and her family moved in with her. Shortly after this in 1937, Moses, Marguerite and Brian moved from Twickenham to Ranelagh Gardens in Fulham.

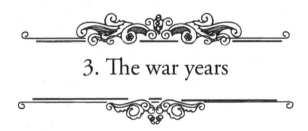

3. The war years

By the outbreak of World War II in 1939,[43] Moses and his family had moved to Fulham, close to the area where Marguerite grew up. We do not know what the family did during World War II. Whilst Moses had served during World War I, firstly aboard the President II at Felixstowe Docks, then transferring to the RAF at Chingford in Essex,[44] no evidence can be found in the war records of him serving in any capacity in the armed forces in World War II. He may however have been in a reserved occupation or have been undertaking approved war work.

Moses would have been thirty-nine years old at the outbreak of war and just below the top age of conscription, which was forty-one. His work as a taxicab driver may have stopped him from being conscripted. The majority of young taxi drivers were called up and there were no new cabs being produced. A large number of taxis and their drivers were requisitioned by the Auxiliary Fire Service to tow trailer pumps and to support the medical services. Some returned to taxi work, but petrol rationing and bomb-damaged streets made the work hard although service men, particularly Americans, provided some custom.[45]

Brian would have been eight years old at the outbreak of war and in the age group to be evacuated under the Government policy to remove children from London, and some other big cities, on the basis that attacks from the Luftwaffe were inevitable and that 'the bomber would always get through'. In the end though, less than half of London's schoolchildren were actually evacuated,[46] and there is no information as to whether or not Brian was one of them.

There are some accounts that Moses and Marguerite had another child, a daughter who was born and died within a day in 1925. If this was the case, perhaps the death of this child made Brian all the more precious to them when he arrived six years later, born to Marguerite after eight years of marriage when she was thirty-two years old. Brian was, to all intents and purposes then, an only child, and both Marguerite and Moses must have had great aspirations for him; and this may have led to tales about an exalted Irish heritage, and stories about Marguerite's family connections to the O'Rourke dynasty in Breffny, Ireland. This could have started a search for this Irish past, becoming something of an obsession with the family.

Means, motive, opportunity

But why, after the war, did the family suddenly leave their home in Fulham and travel to Salt Lake City, Utah, 4,858 miles from their home, on another continent, and to a place where they had no obvious connections? Did the family know that their best option for tracing their family origins might be in the record libraries of the Mormons, held in Salt Lake City, and that to do this they had to convert to the Mormon faith and go there? Moses as a taxi driver may have come into contact with American forces in London during the war who told him about the record libraries, or they may have met Mormons in the area they lived in; we will never know, but they must have started preparations for the journey to Utah by the end of World War II, and this included sorting out issues with their documentation.

It has to be said that being a bit economical with the truth seems to have run in the family, even accounting for the genuine mistakes that sometimes happen when information is given on official forms. There are 'errors' on both Moses and Marguerite's marriage certificate, and on Brian's birth certificate, which meant that formal changes had to be made in 1947 by statutory declarations, both by Moses and

Marguerite, and Moses' mother Rebecca Leese.[47] Moses had called himself Maurice Lees on both documents, and Moses and Marguerite were also listed on their marriage certificate as both being aged 26 when, having been born in 1900, Moses was only 23. Moses' father's name is given as Michael when it was legally Myer. These corrections, in respect of relatively trivial errors, probably had to be made so that Brian and his parents could apply for passports for their trips to America.

Going to America

Brian and his parents converted to Mormonism, travelled to America and joined the Church of Jesus Christ of Latter-day Saints in Salt Lake City, Utah. They travelled on the giant Cunard liner, the Queen Elizabeth, leaving Southampton and bound for New York. Brian left England on 6th May 1949, stating on his immigration forms that his intended future permanent residence would be in the USA.[48]

Landing in New York, he then made his way to Salt Lake City where, on 20th October 1950, he signed and swore a Declaration of Intention to become a citizen of the USA.[49]

Travelling on the Queen Elizabeth to New York to take up a new life was quite some undertaking and would have taken a great deal of the family's resources, perhaps the reason why Brian, just 18 at the time, made this trip alone - a year before his parents, who also travelled on the Queen Elizabeth in 1950. Interestingly, Moses, the taxi driver, put his occupation down as 'chiropodist'.[50]

It is not known whether Moses actually trained as a chiropodist during the war years or in its aftermath, but this is probably yet another untruth to ensure their unobstructed passage to the USA. He certainly didn't practice as a chiropodist while in England or America, and Brian in later years told people that his father was a dentist, and then a medical practitioner - these are just some of the pieces of pedigree burnishing and chicanery that litter this story.

4. A new life in Salt Lake City

Brian worked for several years as a researcher at the Mormon Latter-day Saints (LDS) Genealogical Society in Salt Lake City, becoming a Faculty member there. Not long after he arrived he made a request for church members of Jewish ancestry to contact him so he could compile information about those who had similar ancestry to himself.[51] He began teaching classes on genealogical research,[52] took part in the June Conference Speech Festival,[53] and became a faculty member, conducting 4-day research courses to assist other genealogical workers.[54]

Both Brian and his parents took part in several meetings during 1950 and 1951 where they were introduced as recent converts from England and where they gave testimony about their conversion to Mormonism.[55] Brian was also listed as leaving for France in October 1950, and then for England in November 1950, working as a missionary for the church and was said to be a convert 'of Jewish descent'.[56]

Brian travelled widely in the next few years both for genealogical research purposes and also as a 'Mormon Missionary', and his name on official documents changed several times; on one occasion describing himself as 'Reverend'.[57]

When he first travelled to Utah he was Brian Leese; and he signed as Brian Michael Leese on his application for citizenship. He sailed from New York in January 1951 on the SS America bound for Le Havre. He then left New York on the Queen Elizabeth in December 1952 bound for Southampton, this time calling himself Brian Lees.

In July 1953 he returned to New York on the RMS Mauretania from

Cobh in Ireland, now calling himself Rev. Brian M Leese, with a Salt Lake City address. The title 'Rev.' was completely fictitious, as there is no such title used by the Mormons; similarly his father's use of the title 'Dr' appears to also have been an affectation with no basis in reality.

In between these excursions abroad, Brian returned to Salt Lake City and undertook a variety of teaching and other engagements. In the summer of 1953 he was involved in directing a series of folk festivals with dancing, folk songs and scenes from various countries,[58] and over that winter he taught courses in Los Angeles[59] and then represented the church at a genealogical convention.[60] Between June 1954 and June 1955 he was heavily involved in genealogical courses for their Leadership Week and at conventions where he specialised in Welsh, Irish and Scottish genealogical research.[61]

Moses and Marguerite with the Mormons

There are numerous records in the Salt Lake City Directories and newspaper and periodical articles of Moses and Marguerite's time at the Church of Latter-day Saints between 1951 and 1960,[62] some with Brian and others, latterly, on their own.

All three members of the family became immersed in the Mormon faith: Brian as a genealogical authority and Missionary, and Marguerite as a proof-reader, then a clerk, at the Genealogical Society. Moses worked as a clerk at the Deseret Book store, then with the ZCMI (Zion's Co-operative Mercantile Institution)[63] wholesale pharmaceutical division as a travelling salesman.[64] Moses was definitely not a chiropodist, dentist or any other sort of clinical practitioner during this part of their lives. Moses did however advertise genealogical services in the Deseret News under the name Dr Moses Leese,[65] possibly on behalf of Brian, and was often referred to as Dr Moses Leese in Mormon circles.

Marguerite rapidly became involved in Mormon activities after their arrival in 1951. She spoke at a meeting of the Home Culture Club on the topic 'my testimony' and was described as a 'model and designer

.. recently arrived from London'.[66] She also used her millinery talents, which were said to have been gained when she worked at Harrods in London, to show other women how to make and dress their hats.[67]

Both Moses and Marguerite were active in the social scene and were speakers at the Delta Phi mothers and fathers 1953 Christmas Party;[68] they hosted a meal at their home for a couple going back to Australia and were dinner party guests with five other couples at another couple's home.[69]

1960 is the last time Moses and Marguerite are specifically mentioned as being resident in Salt Lake City, either in the City Directories or newspapers.[70] Where they were living for most of the next 20 years leading up to their deaths in 1980/81 is not known, although they may still have been in SLC in 1969 when Brian gave a lecture there at the World Conference on Records,[71] but for at least part of that time they may have been living in Spain, as will become apparent later in their part of the story.

Brian breaks away

In September 1955 Brian travelled from New York to Plymouth on the liner Isle de France, using a British Passport under the name of Brian M Leese; his occupation is listed at this time as 'none'; his country of permanent residence is listed as USA, and yet his intended duration of stay in the UK is listed as 'indefinite' and he gives a South-West London address not far from his parents old home in Fulham.

Whilst his parents seem to have stayed in Utah, they did return to England at least once in June 1956, flying from Idlewild, New York to London,[72] and for some reason went on to Geneva, Switzerland[73] flying back to New York from there on 15th June.[74] It could be that they left Salt Lake City to see Brian and try to get him back into the fold, but while Brian still kept up his contact with the Mormons for many more years he no longer lived in Salt Lake City or worked at the LDS Genealogical Society.

While Brian's trips during the early to mid-1950s related to his work for the Mormons, he must also have been undertaking research into his own Irish heritage; he definitely visited Ireland,[75] and he met an important contact at the Society of Genealogists in London, Guy Strutt, the son of Robert Strutt, 4th Baron Rayleigh, the renowned physicist. Guy was to become a close friend of Brian's.

Brian never took up his intended US citizenship, his parents were left behind with the Mormons in Utah, and he went on to adopt the name de Breffny. The gradual transformation of identities was taking shape.

1. Poverty in the East End: Gun Street, Spitalfields, 1890. The Leese family lived at 29 Gun Street during the 1870s and 80s, and Myer Leese was born there in 1874.

2. The squalor of Dorset Street in 1903, close to Gun Street, one of the sites of the Jack the Ripper murders. Now demolished.

3. Gravel Lane 1910, looking towards Petticoat Lane Market. Moses and his sister Esther attended Gravel Lane School.

Gravel Lane looking South West 606 11 October 1910

4. Trafalgar School in Twickenham c.1910. the author's grandfather Henry, Moses Leese's younger brother, at school. Back row, third from left.

5. Holidaying in Margate c.1930: Brian's parents Marguerite and Moses Leese (on the left), with his grandparents Rebecca and Myer Leese (on the right).

6. The Leeses on the Prom: Rebecca, Moses, Moses' sister Dorothy and Marguerite.

7. Myer Leese with Brian's cousin Joyce Lees, the author's mother.

9. Holidaying in Southend c.1930: (from the right) Brian's uncle Joe and cousin Joe Jnr, his aunt Dorothy, and cousin Joyce (second from the left).

10. Brian's journey to America: The Queen Elizabeth sailing into New York c.1949.

11. Living with the Mormons in Salt Lake City. Brian's mother Marguerite Leese at a women's meeting in 1951, demonstrating how to refurbish a hat.

12. ZCMI Store, Salt Lake City, where Moses worked as a travelling salesman for the Pharmaceutical Wholesalers in the 1950s.

13. The Mormon Temple, Salt Lake City, Utah.

14. Guy Strutt on the right with his father, Robert Strutt, the 4th Baron Rayleigh, an acclaimed physicist.

15. Sir William and Susana Walton in Ischia, while they were staying at 'Casa Cirillo' in the 1950s.

5. The O'Rourke barony and viscountcy of Breffny

How do the O'Rourkes and the de Breffny titles fit into Brian's story?

Brian's mother, Marguerite and her parents were born in England but her grandparents were Irish – on her father's side from Limerick – and Brian may have been told family stories about connections to the O'Rourkes, although there are no records immediately available of an O'Rourke in the family.

What are the chances?

As a genealogist, Brian would have known that if you look back in any family's history we are all by definition related to thousands of people; all of us have 128 5x great grandparents and 256 6x great grandparents, for example. It is quite likely that Brian may have found some tenuous family connection to the O'Rourkes, and it has been said that whilst researching his mother's Irish ancestry Brian found that one of his great grandmothers' maiden names was Breffni.[76] This gave him the opportunity to weave a new life for himself, elevating the humdrum existence of a taxi driver's son to that of an Irish baron.

Brian researched Irish family history and genealogy in depth as is evident in one of his early books, published in 1974. This work references both the Odell and O'Rourke families in detail,[77] although interestingly he never published an account of his own family genealogical history in this regard, leaving blank how he could possibly have inherited an ancient title passing down through the male line.

A brief history of the O'Rourkes

The O'Rourkes were a famous clan from Irish History. Ruadhrac was King of Breifne, a mediaeval kingdom in Gaelic Ireland[78] in the 9th century, and his descendants, the O'Rourkes, were Princes of Breifne. The last king of West Breifne was Sir Tadhg an Fhiona O Ruairc who died in the latter half of 1605 and he apparently still has living male-line descendants today.[79] There are several branches of the O'Rourke clan, some more senior than others, and this leads to much confusion and debate as to where any legitimate titles should sit, and with which branch of their descendants.

The O'Rourkes resisted the English incursion into Ireland, and many of them fled to Europe when Cromwell confiscated their lands in 1649[80] where they took up various occupations including military service as mercenaries.

There are several conflicting stories about the O'Rourke connection with Russia, and the recognition of the title of 'Count O'Rourke' by the Russian Czars. It is said that Constantine O'Rourke was recognised as Count by the Czarina Elizabeth of Russia on 15th February 1760 (this title was confirmed for his descendants by Nicholas I, on 15th February 1845). The last identifiable heir was Nicholas Nicolaievich O'Rourke, 9th Count O'Rourke, born in 1898, and probably titular 10th Viscount of Breffny and 10th Baron O'Rourke.[81]

Some historians say the Russian branch of the O'Rourke clan was only a minor cadet one, and therefore could not inherit the ancient title. However, it was obviously this version of the origins of the barony that Brian latched on to, as it was said that while in Rome he affected an 'oddly accented English (he took the Russian dimension to the title very seriously)'.[82]

There was of course one major stumbling block to Brian laying any claim to the Irish barony or the Breffny name. Firstly, he would have to prove an ancestral line of descent – and this would have to be through his mother's family (as his father was not Irish, but a London Jew); and as any aristocratic title can only be passed down through the male line, this was a non-starter. How he decided to overcome this seemingly intractable problem becomes apparent later in the story.

His ability to use this flimsy and nebulous aristocratic connection depended on mixing with people who might be impressed by it and which would, by reflection, bring social cachet. His time in Italy would provide the opportunity to use the nebulous aristocratic connection from deep in Ireland's past.

6. The celebrity playground of Ischia

The island of Ischia in the Bay of Naples was developed in the early 1950s by Angelo Rizzoli, a Milanese businessman and successful publisher, who fell in love with its fishing villages and unspoilt landscape. It soon became the playground of the rich and famous. Jet-setting celebrities from the worlds of film, politics and finance[83] holidayed there, with many owning their own private villas.

One such was the English composer Sir William Walton. He and his young wife Susana had met and married in Argentina after knowing each other for just a few weeks. They were a strange couple; she was twenty-two years old and from a well-to-do Argentinian background and he was forty-five. Walton was born and brought up in Oldham in the north-west of England and had by that time had numerous affairs.

Walton informed Susana forcibly on their wedding night that he didn't want children and when she mistakenly became pregnant she had to abide by his decision and have a dangerous backstreet abortion.[84]

He definitely had a penchant for young girls. During island festivities he pinched the bottoms of passing pretty girls and remarked that, far from objecting, they expected such attention.[85] Walton, it is said, 'gave himself permission to behave like a monster on the grounds that he was a genius'.[86]

The Waltons lived in London for some years, visiting Ischia frequently, staying in Casa Cirillo, a wine cellar they converted. Many of their friends visited them there, including Lawrence Olivier and Vivienne Leigh. A number of other artists and authors also frequented the island among them Ibsen, Toscanini, Augustus John, Christopher Isherwood, Truman

Capote and Wystan (WH) Auden, who took a house on the outskirts of Forio[87] with his boyfriend Chester Kallman. Kallman had many young men 'friends' and was a source of scandal on the island, for example organising an orgy while Auden was away, involving a young local man who had sex with everyone who was there, men and women alike.[88]

As the island was developed, many of the painters and writers departed and wealthier visitors arrived: Prince Said ibn Hussein of Jordan bought a house in Forio, millionaire European industrialists, British Peers and a galaxy of film stars and starlets all arrived and it was in this heady mix that Brian found himself - and there he met the Waltons.

William and Susana decided to move permanently to Ischia, and in 1956 bought the land on which they were to build their famous hilltop house 'La Mortella'. While the building work was going on they lived in one of the five cottages they had rebuilt on their land; the others were rented out to help pay for the building of the house.

Harold Acton, Elsa Schiaparelli, Vaughan Williams and his wife, John Ogden and his wife, the ballerina Nadia Nerina, Terence Rattigan, Robin Maughan, Hermione Baddeley, Kay Kendall, Peter Shaffer, Mollie Keane, George Weidenfeld and Sidney Beer were all tenants or invitees of tenants at one time or another as was (unbeknownst to the Waltons) the Nazi war criminal Baldur von Schirach, once head of Hitler's Youth, and Gauleiter of Vienna, who arrived after his release from Spandau Prison.[89]

Von Schirach had during his time in Vienna arranged the deportation of 65,000 Jews from the City and had claimed that this was 'a contribution to European culture'. It is remarkable that the naive Waltons did not recognise the name of a war criminal who had been tried at Nuremberg and imprisoned for his crimes.

La Mortella became a meeting place for their famous (and infamous) friends, a house which in later years Susana was to describe as 'a double prison: he needed me, I needed him'.[90]

Brian, by now calling himself Brian de Breffny, moved to Ischia in 1957[91] no doubt attracted by its reputation as a favourite haunt of the glitterati, and possibly at the instigation of his gay friend Guy Strutt.

Guy's distant relation Harold Acton was a friend of the Waltons, and he may have introduced Brian to them. The Waltons took Brian 'under their wing'[92] and he stayed with them for a year before renting a villa of his own, Casa Montevergine, in Forio just down the hillside from the Waltons.[93]

Brian was bisexual, something that was well known to the Waltons. William Walton once wrote an account of a homosexual orgy at a friend's villa on Ischia that mentioned Brian.[94] As well as his relationship with Guy Strutt, who visited him on his many trips to Italy,[95] Brian also had a relationship with George Mott, an American photographer who, later during the 1970s, collaborated with Brian on many of his books. Mott is quoted as saying that Brian 'never felt comfortable with his homosexuality. He always had to keep up the pretence of being straight',[96] something that would have been important to him if he were to marry and thereby advance his social and financial position.

Although he was by now 'semi-detached' from the Mormons, Brian travelled back to Utah in December 1959 to visit his parents for a month, and while there was the guest lecturer at two public meetings on genealogical research, held in the Logan Tabernacle.[97] It was said that he had spent the past several years abroad on professional genealogical research work.[98]

He flew from Glasgow, Scotland, now calling himself Brian M. Leese de Breffny arriving in New York on the 3rd of December 1959; a few weeks later in February 1960 he left Mexico City on an Air France flight to New York. For both these journeys he had a visa issued in Naples and his stated permanent address was Casa Montevergine, Forio d'Ischia, Italy.[99]

His time in Ischia provided him with huge opportunities to meet and ingratiate himself with the rich and the famous including many actors and minor royals who moved in the same circles and visited the Waltons. He made several flamboyant acquaintances there including the Princess del Drago, known as Mimosa, and her sister Princess Carla of Orleans-Bourbon,[100] Princess Maria Pia of Bourbon Palma – and another one of the people he met was a young and impressionable Princess Jyotsna of Burdwan.

7. A secret marriage to an Indian princess

Within a few months of meeting the twenty-three-year-old Princess Jyotsna Devi Mahtab of Burdwan, Brian, twenty-nine at the time, had proposed to her. They left Ischia for England and were married (after five days of hiding in secrecy)[101] on 24th September 1960 in a civil ceremony at the Register Office in Bridgnorth, Shropshire. The marriage was a rushed and secret affair to ensure that Jyotsna's parents could not stop it. Once the press got wind of the marriage, reporters were told there was no information to be given about the wedding.[102]

At the time of the marriage the couple were staying at Aldenham Park, the substantial country home of Baron Acton and his wife Daphne, Guy Strutt's sister. Guy and his mother Kathleen were both witnesses at the wedding along with Karuna Mahtab, Princess Jyotsna's younger sister. However, neither Jyotsna's nor Brian's parents were present.

Jyotsna was the daughter of Sir Uday Chand Mahtab the Maharajadhiraja Bahadur of Bardhaman Raj, K.C.I.E.[103] He was the last ruler of Burdwan Raj and one of the richest princes in India until 1955 when the Zamindari system[104] was abolished.

Princess Jyotsna's mother, the Maharanee of Burdwan, rushed to England to take her daughter home as the marriage, it was said, 'would be against Calcutta State laws'. However, she was too late to prevent it as she didn't arrive in the country until Saturday 1st October. Apparently, the Maharajah and Marharanee 'did not even know the name of the young man'[105] their daughter was to marry.

Brian's penchant for deception extended to his marriage certificate. He must have been economical with the truth about his family background to Princess Jyotsna, because of her status and who her parents were. At this point Brian was calling himself Brian Michael O'Dell Leese de Breffny and describing himself as a man of 'independent means'.

He said on the marriage certificate that his father was Maurice Michael Leese de Breffny whose rank quite unbelievably (given that his father was Jewish) was stated as Baron de Breffny[106] of 'independent means',[107] an Irish title Brian was soon to take for himself, long before his father was dead. This demonstrates clearly the bogus nature of his claim to the barony - as at this time his father was in Salt Lake City, working as a travelling salesman for the ZCMI Mormon store.

Brian and Jyotsna returned to Ischia to live, although they were back in London for the birth of their daughter Sita-Maria Arabella on 4th July 1962 at 27 Welbeck Street - a top private hospital close to Harley Street in central London's hub of private healthcare.[108] Sir William Walton became her godfather[109] and she was named after her godmother, Princess Maria Pia,[110] and Brian now styled himself 'baron' on his daughter Sita's birth certificate.[111]

Sita has a very different and more romantic view of her parents' marriage, no doubt the 'official version' imparted to her by Brian. Sita says that after the two met in Italy, Brian followed Jyotsna to Calcutta where they were married at Jyotsna's parents' house.[112] This is nothing but a convenient fantasy story as it is quite clear that Jyotsna's parents disapproved of the marriage and tried to stop it.

Brian and Jyotsna's marriage didn't last long. They had gone to live in Rome and a year after Sita's birth, just 3 years into the marriage, Jyotsna left Italy leaving Brian to bring up their daughter alone. Shortly after their separation Jyotsna filed for divorce; but Brian defended the suit and contested her right to file for divorce in London on the basis of jurisdiction, by questioning the address she had given in the UK as her permanent residence.[113] She was in the end granted a decree nisi in the London Divorce Court in July 1968 citing the adultery of her husband as the cause.[114]

Perhaps Brian continued his relationships with Guy Strutt and George Mott, both of whom he was in close touch with, or had relationships with other women - we shall never know. In one newspaper report it said that they both admitted adultery and that Brian, currently living in Rome, won custody of their daughter Sita.[115] He left the marriage with what has been described as a more than generous divorce settlement from Jyotsna.[116] Perhaps she would have been well advised to have looked more closely at her marriage certificate and seen the falsehoods it contained.

Jyotsna went on to remarry twice, having a son with Anthony Mayer, whom she later divorced, and then marrying Ashish Ranjan Dutt. She died in November 2009.

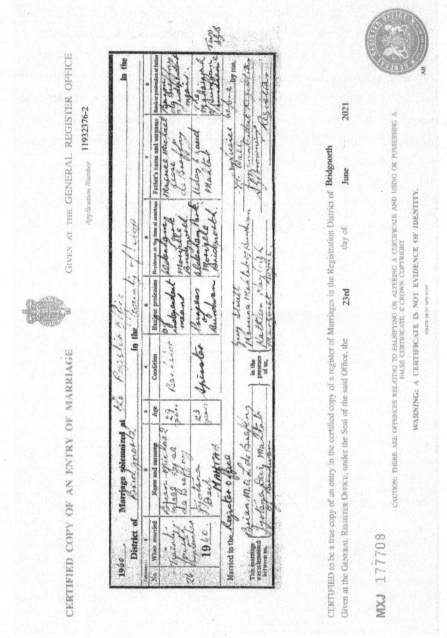

16. © Crown Copyright. Brian and Jyotsna's Marriage Certificate showing Brian's father as Maurice Michael Leese de Breffny (his name was actually Moses Leese) and his occupation as Baron de Breffny of independent means, when in 1960 he was in Salt Lake City working as a travelling salesman for the Mormons.

8. The glamour of life in Rome

After the breakup of his marriage to Jyotsna, Brian strove to live a life of luxury with his daughter in a large apartment at Via Frattina 10, near the Spanish Steps in Rome. Via Frattina was at this time a small street with a few shops including 'a gilder and frame maker, a greengrocer, a corset shop and a shop that sold nothing but chicken breasts'.[117] They had Indian servants – who apparently wore turbans and flowing white robes[118] - and a nanny for Sita, while Brian worked.[119]

Sita talks of having a colourful international upbringing surrounded by the elegance of her 'parents palace'.[120] Her grandparents' real palace in India had by this time been confiscated and handed over to the University of Burdwan, and it is quite clear that Brian and Jyotsna didn't have a palace anywhere in the short time they were together, unless the apartment in Rome was considered a 'palace' by a young Sita when she was living there.

In the early years in Rome Brian ran a business tracing family and ancestral pedigrees[121] using the research skills he had acquired during his time in Salt Lake City, and this may well have brought him into contact with many rich and famous people during this iconic period.

It was the Rome of Federico Fellini, 'La Dolce Vita'[122] and was enjoyed by Italian film stars and Hollywood royalty working in Rome at the time; stars such as Brigitte Bardot, Audrey Hepburn, Raquel Welch and Marcello Mastroianni, Sophia Loren, Richard Burton and Liz Taylor,[123] were there, as well as many dispossessed members of European Royalty. Rome was thought to be the coolest city on earth with the Via Veneto, just a few minutes from the Via Frattina where Brian lived, being the centre of international high society after-dark activities. It boasted such glamorous locations as a Harry's Bar and a Café de Paris.

However, Brian remained in contact with the Mormons. He was still being called 'a convert from England' by them and was reported as having undertaken special research assignments for the Church for several years. He was also working with an organisation called the Irish Research Committee (IRC) in Winchester Street, London[124] as Committee Chair, along with Guy Strutt and George Mott who were vice-chairmen.[125]

Brian appears to have blotted his copybook while working with the IRC. It was reported that he had gone to Ireland 'and by patiently searching old parish registers he uncovered information on sixteen sets of great-grandparents for a (Mormon) Salt Lake City woman'.[126] However, an article about the Little family's history and the research done by the Little sisters says that 'to help them these ladies employed a professional genealogist, Mr Leese of the Irish Research Committee ….. Later they fell out with him claiming that he had not visited some of the places (in Ireland) on which he had reported!'.[127]

In 1969 Brian and Guy Strutt gave a public lecture in the Logan Tabernacle and attended the World Conference on Records in Salt Lake City.[128] It is not clear if this was the only time Guy Strutt visited Salt Lake City with Brian, and although there are no records to verify this, Brian's parents may still have been living there as late as 1969 because Strutt talked of travelling to Salt Lake City with Brian and speaking to his father on the phone, although he said he was not allowed to meet Brian's parents in person.[129]

Brian was obviously trying by this time to hide his parents true identities. Indeed, he apparently assured his friend the author Muriel Spark[130] that his 'stepfather' was a top dentist in Salt Lake City,[131] a version of a story which was to reappear much later in his life to try to explain his claim to the de Breffny title.

Deception and falsehood

During this time Brian began to embellish the stories about his life and lineage. He had no formal higher education – there is no evidence that he ever attended any University as a student. He left London at the age of eighteen, the normal age to enter University education, and went to live in Salt Lake City where he became a Mormon. For several years he was a researcher and lecturer at the Mormon Latter-day Saints Genealogical Society where his mother was a proof-reader and his father worked for the Mormon department store, the ZCMI,[132] firstly as a stock counter and following that as a travelling salesman in the pharmaceutical wholesalers. Brian also spent time travelling as a Mormon missionary and called himself on occasion 'Reverend'.[133]

He began to distance himself from his Mormon past and told stories of having been to Oxford or the Sorbonne or the University of Utah, and indeed as the dust jacket on one of his books claims he was: 'Educated at the University of Paris and Stanford University, California'.[134] He presumably felt that he had to invent an academic background to lend weight to the image of himself, and to give credence to his genealogical work and the historical research he undertook for the books he was to write. There is no evidence that he studied at any of these academic institutions, either as an undergraduate or postgraduate.

There were also numerous tall tales of other aspects of his life that were told to various acquaintances. He said he was brought up in France under German occupation (when he would have been nine and would have had to emigrate from Britain to occupied France, an impossibility), been a barman in Mexico, and an interpreter at the United Nations, amongst other bizarre claims.[135]

The deceptions continued. The Metropolitan Museum of Art in New York held an exhibition of medieval Irish art in October 1977 which Brian attended, with copies of two of his books: the recently published 'The Irish World' and 'Castles of Ireland'.

He was interviewed by the arts writer for Westchester Rockland Newspapers who understood him to be Baron Brian de Breffny 'whose title comes from an old principality in Northwest Ireland' and he told her his family name was O'Rorke, that he was born in France and educated at the Sorbonne. He also told a story about his eighty-four-year-old mother, who would actually have been eighty-one at this time,[136] and who in fact died aged eighty-four in 1980.

Guy Strutt said Brian was far from honest, and that he had once been double-crossed by him[137] which seems a very kind way of saying he was an inveterate cheat and liar; but despite all that Guy remained a friend and colleague of his until Brian's death in 1989.

A dalliance with Muriel Spark

Muriel Spark, most famously known for her novel 'The Prime of Miss Jean Brodie', moved to Rome from New York in 1967 having abandoned Britain forever to get away as she put it 'from old friends from whom her sudden success had estranged her'.

Being in Rome allowed Muriel to indulge her love of stylish living and balance a lifestyle of parties with her writing.[138] She had 'reinvented herself as a chic and super-successful lady with perfect hair and 'maquillage', expensive jewellery, furs, an apartment …just across the road from the Vatican, handy for symposia with the curia and nobles and Cinecitta film types who she numbered among her glittering friends'.[139] And one of these friends was Brian de Breffny, as he was now known.

Brian met Muriel Spark in about 1970 at Queen Frederica of Greece's house in Rome.[140] Their friendship apparently grew after this meeting when Brian phoned her professing to love her work, and they developed a close relationship which lasted for several years. Indeed, it is said that they were 'intermittently' lovers.[141] Brian's daughter Sita tells of glamorous dinner parties in her father's house in the Via Frattina with diverse celebrities including Muriel Spark and Queen Frederica of Greece.[142]

However, while Brian and Muriel may have been 'intermittently lovers' Brian was also continuing his gay relationships. Penelope Jardine, Muriel's erstwhile Secretary who became her life-long companion, said

17. Polo at Ranelagh in south-west London, May 1928. Jyotsna's father, Maharajah Kumar Uday Chand Mahtab (right) and next to him her grandfather the Maharajah of Burdwan.

18. Aldenham House, the country home of Baron Acton, where Brian and Jyotsna hid themselves away before they were married.

18. Princess Jyotsna leaving the Divorce Court in 1968 after being granted her Decree Nisi.

19. Sophia Loren in 1963 leaving the hairdressers and crossing Via Frattina, where Brian and his daughter Sita lived while in Rome.

19. Muriel Spark, author of 'The Prime of Miss Jean Brodie' and close friend of Brian's in Rome.

20. Queen Frederica of Greece, who lived in exile in Rome following the 1967 coup. Brian met Muriel Spark at Queen Frederica's house and the Queen attended dinner parties at his house in the Via Frattina.

21. Brian in the 1960s in Italy.

22. The book launch of 'The Irish World' in 1976. Brian (far right) and co-author Rosemary ffoliott (second left).

23. The British Colonial Hotel in Bay Street, Nassau, where Stafford Sands hosted a banquet for travel agents in 1961.

24. Stafford Sands (left) discussing the economic development of the Bahamas with Hitler's money man Hjalmar Schacht in 1962.

25. Hitler's henchman Otto Skorzeny, husband of Ilse Skorzeny. Ilse Skorzeny was the Foreign Investment Promoter for Grand Bahama and Stafford Sands' companion when he visited Germany.

26. Syndicate boss and casino money man Meyer Lansky, who bankrolled the Bahamas casinos, being taken to jail in Florida on drugs charges in 1970.

27. Recently married Sir Stafford and Lady Ulli Sands at a banquet in 1966, with Ulli in a brocade dress and white mink capelet.

28. Bahamian banknote with portrait of Stafford Sands, on a pile of US dollars.

29. The Villa Corner della Regina in the Veneto, Italy, bought by Sir Stafford Sands, where he and Ulli (Lady Sands) lived after they fled the Bahamas.

that Muriel was keen to know everybody and maybe meet another interesting man but that there were 'too many homosexuals around'[143] and some of her closest companions were homosexual males: Eugene Walter, Dario Ambrosiani, Brian de Breffny and Count Lanfranco Rasponi and also Brian's gay friends, the Honourable Guy Strutt and George Mott. She apparently felt closest to bluffers and imposters and charmers and acolytes, encouraging them to struggle for her preference.[144]

Ambrosiani disliked Brian and said 'he was a man who played both sides of the street. He went after rich women but he also had a boyfriend'.[145]

In 1972 Muriel accompanied Brian and George Mott on a month-long trip to Ireland. The purpose of the trip was for Brian to research a book he was to write with Rosemary ffolliot - 'The Houses of Ireland' - and for George Mott to take the photographs for it. The trip lasted about a month with Muriel having found a place to stay and buying a car, which Brian and George drove around in order to examine houses and landscapes.[146]

Muriel also went to India with Brian in 1973, along with Guy Strutt, George Mott, and 'Brian's elderly 'godmother' Souny, Comtesse G. de Tonnac-Villeneuve,' mainly to go to the wedding of Brian's Indian cook in Trivandrum. They travelled via Delhi to Trivandrum and then as far as Sri Lanka visiting temples and rock sculptures.[147]

By the 1970s Brian's attraction to religion had been transferred from the Mormons to Catholicism, possibly in order to buttress his pretence at being a member of the Irish aristocracy. Both Brian and George Mott were votaries of the Charismatic Renewal, a Pentecostal movement of the Catholic Church in Rome. Muriel, who had converted to Catholicism herself in 1954, went to a lot of meetings although she was apparently only amused by it and distant.[148]

Brian and Muriel's relationship waned in 1976 when Muriel found out that Brian had met the very rich, beautiful and widowed Lady Ulli Sands and that his affections had therefore turned elsewhere.

Although her relationship with Brian had ended, Muriel remained close to both Guy Strutt, who became a life-long friend,[149] and George Mott, as well as Brian's daughter Sita, and for many years attended dinner parties with them.

9. A Finnish heiress, the Nazis and the Mafia

So who was Lady Ulli Sands? Ulli (née Castren) married Sir Stafford Lofthouse Sands in December 1965. They were married for just six years before Sir Stafford Sands died in 1972, leaving Ulli immensely rich.

Ulli was born on 6th December 1919 in Helsingfors, Finland. She was a beautiful, well-travelled woman who had multiple relationships with men in quick succession. She was married four times: her first marriage was to Ake Lillas with whom she had four children; a second marriage which apparently lasted only a few months; a third was to Sir Stafford Lofthouse Sands, and lastly to Brian Leese who was by this time calling himself Baron de Breffny. As well as her four marriages Ulli is said to have had a number of affairs, most notably with Sir Peter Rawlinson MP, the British Attorney General, and also with a Finnish Prime Minister.[150]

When Sir Stafford Sands died he left Ulli a huge inheritance; but where did the money come from?

The scandal of Sir Stafford Lofthouse Sands and his millions

The Bahamas, still a British colony during the 1950s and 60s, is an archipelago of 700 islands 181 miles off the Florida coast. The colony was run by a tight clique of old white families who dominated the Government and Island commerce, despite black people being a considerable majority of the population. The members of the ruling clique were known as the Bay Street Boys – named after the street where their offices were, and close to the luxurious estates where they lived.

The most influential of the clique was the United Bahamian Party grandee, and Government Minister of Finance and Tourism, Sir Stafford Lofthouse Sands - a multimillionaire lawyer, gourmet, collector of antique paperweights and Yankee dollars. Nothing involving money in the Bahamas took place without the consent and support of Sands, who extracted whopping legal fees for 'services' to facilitate deals and transactions.[151]

Stafford Sands represented Nassau City in Parliament and was first elected as an MP in the Bahamas in January 1937, two years later becoming legal adviser to Parliament. When the colony became self-governing in 1964, Sir Stafford became a Cabinet Minister[152] and did much to develop tourism and turn the Bahamas into a financial centre. However, this was achieved through a number of illegal methods to swerve round existing laws and bring in unsavoury figures to complete the projects.

Out and out electoral corruption was also involved: Sir Randol Fawkes[153] said that Sands wined and dined black Bahamians in his palatial East Bay Street mansion and on his yacht 'The Enchantress' during each election cycle,[154] to curry favour and gain votes for his white dominated Party, and maintain control of Parliament, despite the black majority amongst those entitled to vote.

Sands set about creating a superior tourist product during the 1950s and 60s. He had become chairman of the Bahamas Development Board, opening offices in Nassau, Miami, Chicago, Dallas, Montreal, London and New York,[155] giving banquets to travel agents in the British Colonial Hotel in Nassau,[156] parties at Claridge's in London,[157] and travelling to Miami to give speeches on how the Bahamas had developed its tourism industry.[158] His key role was, however, to involve himself in the development of casinos, gambling, and all the associated 'services' running alongside the hotels, services for which he received huge sums of money.

Gambling was illegal in the Bahamas, with the exception of a seasonal gambling club operating for only three months a year. In the mid-1950s Stafford Sands, along with a swindler from Baltimore, Wallace Groves, applied for government grants to create Freeport, a free trade zone where businesses paid no taxes, and will not until the year 2054.[159] However, in 1962 it became apparent that the Freeport area needed new and attractive features which would encourage the injection of capital by investors, and a casino was suggested as the central feature of the development.

Stafford Sands had tried some years earlier to get the 'Certificates of Exemption' legislation[160] extended, without success, but now hatched a plan to ensure that an application would succeed this time. A company called Bahamas Amusements Ltd was formed by Stafford Sands with Groves and a conman friend of his, Lou Chesler, and the same day that the Company was formed an application for a Certificate of Exemption, drafted by Stafford Sands, was lodged in secret, and away from Parliamentary scrutiny. The certificate was granted and the Amusements company obtained the rights to operate an unlimited number of casinos on Grand Bahama for a period of ten years.[161]

The Nazi connection

The development of the Bahamas turned not just on casinos but also on the 'parking' of offshore funds that would escape American and British taxation, the laundering of gambling and drug money, all of which needed legal, property and staffing advice from well-placed people in the Bahamas.

For these major developments heavy-hitter support was needed. Sands turned to Hjalmar Schacht, in the 1960s an adviser on economic development, but who had previously served in Hitler's administration as President of the Reichsbank from 1933-39, and Minister for the Economy until 1937. Schacht had converted to fascism after reading Hitler's autobiography 'Mein Kampf' in 1930. In these key financial positions, he had the roles of ending rampant inflation, financing post-depression reconstruction, and funding the great Nazi armaments drive, using circuitous methods to circumvent international Treaties.[162]

Schacht co-operated with Hitler for many years, but in 1944 was arrested by the Gestapo for allegedly having contact with the assassins, led by Von Stauffenberg,[163] who attempted to kill Hitler.

Schacht was put on trial after 1945 by the Allied Powers at the Nuremburg military tribunals, which used both military and international law to prosecute key figures in the Nazi regime. Schacht was fully acquitted but then re-arrested by the Germans on other charges.

In 1955 he founded a private banking house and advised developing countries on economic development, which is undoubtedly how he came into contact with Stafford Sands in 1962. We know that Sands toured Europe in that year to promote the Bahamas[164] and whilst there, had a long conversation with Schacht in Germany who was then invited back to the Bahamas to 'study the potential'.[165]

Schacht's advice on economic development was enhanced by an even more extraordinary figure, that of Ilse Skorzeny, Schacht's niece, and the wife of Hitler's pet kidnapper Otto Skorzeny.[166] Ilse had married Skorzeny in 1953 and they lived in Madrid until Otto died from cancer in 1975.

Ilse undertook many promotional trips across Europe as a Foreign Investment Promoter of Grand Bahama on behalf of Sands, and the Bahamas casino/tourism projects in the early 1960s,[167] and it is possible that the Skorzenys provided a safe haven for Sands in Spain when he had to evacuate the Bahamas quickly after his activities were exposed.

The Mafia take control

If the former Nazis Schacht and Skorzeny were key in unlocking access to funds and promoting gambling and tourism, the management of the new casinos was recruited from the American 'syndicate'; men who had been involved in illegal gambling and huge amounts of money laundering in the United States, and who had recently been expelled from Cuba, following the 1959 Castro revolution there.

Sands' operation on the islands was not just to create a new casino industry, but to link in to one of the first 'offshore banking' facilities in the world in Switzerland – Banque International de Credit - set up by Tibor Rosenbaum, a shady character with Mossad connections, who later opened a local subsidiary in Freeport called Atlas Bank. The casino skim from Vegas now mingled with casino skim from the Bahamas and moved through Bahamian banks on its way to Switzerland.[168]

Despite efforts in the Bahamas to exclude American employees from working in the new Casinos, it was easy for the syndicate mobsters to put in their own people to run things for them[169] and one such was Dino Cellini, an employee of Meyer Lansky who bankrolled the casino.[170] Lansky was one of the richest and most powerful US crime syndicate bosses (along with Mafia bosses Lucky Luciano and Johnny Torio), who specialised in providing banking facilities to launder funds through foreign accounts.[171] Lansky was also credited with using blackmail to gain influence with politicians, policemen and judges.[172] The character of Hyman Roth in the film 'The Godfather part II' is widely accepted to be based on Lansky.

However, things did not run smoothly for Sands, as his Party lost control of the Bahamian Government in 1967, thus enabling political opponents to initiate investigations into his activities, and he bolted from the Bahamas and went to Spain.

By this time, Sands was in deep trouble and was required to appear as a witness in front of a Royal Commission[173] which was sent from London to 'air the dirty linen of the colony's politics'.[174] Stafford Sands took his time before he returned to the Bahamas to face the Commission where he had to explain why he had been paid $1.8m in fees (equivalent to a buying power of $14.74m in 2021 terms), by the operators of two lavish and controversial casinos. The money had apparently changed hands both before and after the Certificates of Exemption were granted by the Government, in which Sands was himself Minister of Finance.[175]

The Royal Commission recorded that Meyer Lansky visited the Bahamas and offered Stafford Sands $2 million to allow casino gambling. Sands told the Commission he had rejected the bribe, although it was revealed that both Lansky and his associate Morris Lansburgh, the corrupt Miami Beach hotel owner, had links with the Bay Street Boys in the Bahamas. Sands was, however, able to hold on to his money – by escaping from the Bahamas to Spain, he ensured that he held on to his huge fortune which amounted to $55m (equivalent to £291m in 2021).

Shortly afterwards, Sir Stafford and Ulli (Lady Sands) went to live in one of Italy's grand palazzos in Cavasagra di Vedelago in the province of Treviso, Italy, 35 kilometres from Venice. The sixteenth century, thirty-seven room Villa Corner della Regina, was purchased 'with his corruptly gotten millions' by Sir Stafford in 1968.[176] He restored the palazzo and added a swimming pool with hydromassage and tennis courts[177] and used it to entertain 'such luminaries as Maria Callas, John Paul Getty and the Rockefellers'.[178]

How much did Ulli know?

Ulli must have known of the corruption and backhanders that got Sands his money. She married him in 1965 at the height of his questionable financial dealings. She was an intelligent woman and socialised with the nefarious people Sands mixed with in the Bahamas.

Sands and Ulli hosted a party of attendees at the opening of the 'Bahamian Club' in West Bay Street, 'Nassau's only casino supper club', a club in which Mrs Wallace Groves 'has an interest', and the Groves' flew in from Grand Bahama for the occasion.[179] Ulli is described as 'blonde Junoesque Lady Sands, the recent bride of Sir Stafford Sands, … in a fitted gown of white and beige brocade topped with a white mink caplet'.[180]

She was certainly aware of his appearance at the hearings of the Royal Commission. She returned to the Bahamas from Spain with Stafford Sands when he attended the hearings,[181] and will have heard all the evidence about the money he took and how he tried to influence votes.[182]

Perhaps she tried to keep herself well away from it all and turned a blind eye. However, she benefitted greatly as almost all Sands' fortune was left to her in a rather curious Will that stipulated she be paid a fixed income, linked to inflation, even though it might exhaust the estate;[183] however this would have taken some doing given the size of his fortune.

Presumably his money, corruptly gained and enabled by former Nazi advisers and Mafia crooks, was salted away in the offshore tax havens used to hide the casino money before they left the Bahamas; and this no doubt provided the investment pot from which Ulli's huge income was paid - which of course also benefitted Brian greatly when he married her.

Sands was an out and out crook. He used his position as Finance Minister in the Bahamian Government to obtain huge personal advantage, bribed thousands of black Bahamians to vote for his Party to maintain it in power, linked up with Nazis and the Mafia, and hightailed it when things got rough in the late 1960s. His face is on the Bahamian $10 bill, and his fortune was intact when he died in 1972 in London's Dorchester Hotel. Ulli was the long-term beneficiary – and so by definition was Brian de Breffny.

Brian meets Ulli – and her fortune

Brian met Ulli in Italy and they were married in 1976 just four years after the death of Stafford Sands, and it was only in that same year that Muriel Spark found out that Brian had a new love in his life.

Once married, they began to look for a place in Ireland where they could spend a few months a year.[184] They found the rather rundown Castletown Cox, a very substantial Palladian country house in County Kilkenny, with 513 acres of surrounding estate, 36,000 sq. feet and four floors of house, a lake, a 400 metre long ha-ha, gardens and farmland, and moved there in 1978.[185] Castletown Cox is a distinguished eighteenth century building in the Italian tradition, and certainly one of the most desirable in Ireland.

Although she was eleven years older than Brian, Ulli lived for a further twenty-two years after he died from cancer, aged just fifty-eight, in 1989; their married life only lasted for thirteen years. But during that time, her inherited millions enabled an expensive glitterati lifestyle for them both, which would be the envy of top Irish society. The contrast with Brian's humble beginnings as the son of a Jewish taxi driver from Twickenham could hardly be starker.

After staying on for some years at Castletown Cox after Brian's death, Ulli sold up and moved to a Dublin townhouse before eventually moving to Gozo, Malta, in 2004, dying there on 5th September 2011 at the age of ninety.

10. A lavish life in a Palladian mansion

Brian and Ulli called themselves Baron and Baroness de Breffny[186] in a bizarre show of elitism to fit the Palladian Mansion they lived in. They threw extravagant house-parties for their rich and famous guests who included numerous members of the aristocracy, ambassadors and glitterati.

Their visitors included Miranda and Benjamin Guinness, Molly Keane, Eleanor Lambert, Terry Keane and Sybil Connolly and old friends such as Guy Strutt, George Mott and the Waltons, who spent a week with Brian and Ulli at Castletown Cox in 1982 to avoid William, who was ill, becoming exhausted by his fans and friends in London.[187]

On hearing of William's death in 1983, George Mott rushed to Ischia to help, and Brian helped with funeral arrangements in Florence before returning to 'La Mortella' with Susana to address hundreds of envelopes for her thank-you letters.[188] Brian and his daughter Sita also attended the ceremony in Ischia when William Walton's ashes were interred.[189]

When Susana Walton wrote her biography of William Walton in 1988 she wrote in her acknowledgements: 'I gratefully acknowledge the assistance … of Brian de Breffny for a lifetime of friendship, a colossal memory reviving scenes of our younger days in Forio, and most particularly for his generosity and kindness in extensively editing my corrected draft'.[190]

The de Breffny house parties at Castletown Cox lasted for days: a kitchen supper for fourteen on the Friday, black tie dinner on Saturday night, and formal luncheon on Sunday[191] with huge amounts of champagne and caviar, during which the servants witnessed decadence on an epic scale.[192] There were beeswax candles and lilies on display, musicians playing in the great stone-flagged hall and Indian servants to gratify every whim.

At these events the indiscretions of Irish society were maximised, marriages were broken, matches were made and divorces became absolute. It was said that it would not be uncommon for a woman to find her earrings in two separate bedrooms.[193] Brian's gay affairs continued during this decadent time and Ulli apparently gave large sums of money to at least two of his lovers when the affairs were over.[194]

All this was funded from what was left of Brian's divorce settlement, and of course the Stafford Sands money that Ulli had inherited, derived from her late husband's illicit casino operations and mob connections.

Brian and Ulli were not the only ones throwing lavish dinner parties in their stately homes. They went to a dinner party at Birr Castle, the home of the 7th Earl of Rosse, in 1981 which was filmed for the pilot of an RTE television programme called 'Stately Meals': however, this rather distasteful production, when viewed in the context of the history of Ireland, was never broadcast. Other guests at this meal included the royal photographer Lord Lichfield, Princess Harshad Purna Devi of Mori and her husband Garech de Brun.

Given the opulence of their lifestyle and lavish overindulgence at their Castletown Cox parties, it was incredible that Brian, towards the end of his life, had the audacity to write a letter to one of Dublin's newspapers, criticising their journalist Terry Keane for spending £120 on a dinner for two, and calling it 'sheer vulgarity' to write about 'one's excesses'.[195] Presumably as long as you don't write about it, 'excess' isn't vulgar.

Castletown Cox reborn

Brian said that he and Ulli fell in love with Castletown Cox on the day they first saw it. It was 'magnificent in its discreet unlaboured elegance, the sun dappling the slated domes over the twin pavilions and casting long shadows through the branches of the centuries-old beeches along the avenue'.[196] The house had a grandiose hall with giant fluted Corinthian columns, lovely rococo plasterwork and 24 spacious rooms. They originally turned their backs on the house, daunted at the prospect of restoring and maintaining it,[197] but eventually took the plunge and bought it in 1978.

Nearly 300 of Ireland's 'Big Houses' were destroyed during what is called the 'Irish Revolutionary Period'[198] when they were burned down, blown up or wrecked by the IRA[199] who hoped these actions would overcome the culture of deference towards the landowning class. Some were also targeted to deny them as billeting for British forces, or as reprisals for house burnings by British forces.

Most of these large country houses belonged to the Anglo-Irish aristocracy, Unionists, or suspected informers and were seen as symbols of the oppression of the majority Roman Catholic population.

When Brian first moved to Ireland, he stayed in Castletown Conolly and then Leixlip Castle, both of which were owned by Desmond and Mariga Guinness. He joined Guinness and Desmond Fitzgerald[200] in working enthusiastically to protect Irish architecture and heritage at a time when most Irish people still felt antagonism or indifference towards the great houses, and as a consequence many were left as ruins or demolished.

Brian and Ulli worked to turn Castletown Cox back into one of the stately homes of Ireland. It was originally built between 1767 and 1771 for Michael Cox, the Archbishop of Castel, and after several other owners it was finally sold to Brian and Ulli, who are credited with saving the house, with its façade of dressed sandstone and Kilkenny marble, from the dilapidation they found it in.

Brian mentioned Castletown Cox in one of his books 'The Houses of Ireland' saying 'Indeed, two of Ireland's loveliest surviving country houses were built to (Ducart's) designs – Castletown Cox, Co. Kilkenny …' It was also illustrated in 'Irish Houses and Castles';[201] featured in 'In the Houses of Ireland'[202] and Castletown Cox's extensive grand, formal gardens were included in a book entitled 'In an Irish Garden' in 1986.[203]

When Castletown Cox was sold in 1990 by Ulli after Brian's death, it realised the sum of £2m and the contents sold for a further £552,000.[204] There were 1,000 lots in the Christie's sale including pictures, furniture, prints and sculpture brought from Italy.[205]

Castletown Cox was bought by Merchant Banker George Magan, the Treasurer of the British Conservative Party, Tory member of the House of Lords, and a Deputy Governor of the Bank of Ireland. He undertook a major restoration of the house, wings and pavilion, and filled it with paintings and other treasures.

Magan was said to be worth '£200 million' and the great mansion was filled with £30 million of old masters; but by 2020 the house was sold from underneath him by the Jersey Trust he himself had set up for the benefit of his children, because of unpaid rent,[206] and in 2020 he was declared bankrupt. He had to sell his £6m home in Kensington and his wife divorced him, alleging that he had concealed important financial documents.

11. Sita-Maria and a royal connection

Brian's daughter Sita-Maria lived with him at Castletown Cox, and during that time met her future husband Thomas Vesey, 7th Viscount di Vesci, the son of Susan Anne Armstrong-Jones,[207] who was a frequent visitor to the house. The de Vesci titles and peerage go back to the seventeenth century when the baronetcy was first created in 1698, with the barony being created in 1750.

Thomas Vesey is the nephew of Anthony Armstrong-Jones, 1st Earl Snowdon, who was the former husband of Queen Elizabeth II's sister, Princess Margaret. The 6th Viscount di Vesci's home, Abbeyleix, was a favourite haunt of Lord Snowdon and Princess Margaret during the time they were married in the 1960s,[208] as Lord Snowdon was the brother of the then Viscountess de Vesci, and Princess Margaret spent her 32nd birthday there.

On one occasion whilst the royal pair were visiting on holiday there was an attack by the IRA. Ten men were detained after an explosion near Abbeyleix House which blew in some windows and plunged the house into darkness.[209] The executive of the Belfast Republican Directorate then condemned the Dublin Government for protecting the 'Royal representatives of a hostile foreign power'.[210]

Sita became pregnant and had Thomas Vesey's child in 1985, and they were engaged to be married eighteen months later. Her father, Brian, was quick to declare that Viscount di Vesci had recognised the child, and it was registered as his. He said that the delay in the marriage was to make sure of the couple's feelings as they were both practicing

Catholics.[211] They eventually had three children together.

Sita and Thomas Vesey were married on 5th September 1987. Brian must have been overjoyed by this aristocratic union and spared no expense for his daughter's wedding, including sending a questionnaire out with the wedding invitations, asking guests from across Europe what type of transport they needed him to provide for them to get there.[212] Sita wore a 'wonderful gown' made for her by Ib Jorgensen, a top Irish fashion designer.[213]

The wedding took place in the church of the Assumption, Templeorum, County Kilkenny and was attended by Lord Snowdon along with 400 people who gathered in the village for this 'high society' event.[214] When Princess Margaret's son Viscount Linley married in 1993, Sita's daughter Cosima was one of the bridesmaids.

Goodbye to Abbeyleix

After their marriage Sita and her husband lived on his family 2,000-acre estate, Abbeyleix, with its fifty-seven rooms, in County Laois, Eire. The house with its mile long drive had been in the family for 300 years. They employed a nanny for the children having advertised for a nanny/housekeeper with a knowledge of Indian culture and ability to prepare Indian dishes.[215] However, just three years after their marriage Thomas Vesey had to put the house on the market and auction off all its contents.

Following his father's death, there were inheritance tax obligations amounting to over £1 million, which Thomas Vesey could not pay without liquidating substantial assets. Attempts were made to save the house by Thomas and Sita and by Thomas' uncle, the Earl of Rosse. Thomas tried to get a tax arrangement with the Irish Government, similar to the National Trust in Great Britain, where ownership would be vested in the State while the family still occupied the house and opened it to the public, but this was not possible.[216]

The house went on the market with a price in excess of £4 million

32. Ulli and Brian at one of their lavish parties.

33. Castletown Cox in 1983 during the time Brian and Ulli lived there.
© photographer Derry Moore

34. The grand entrance hall of Castletown Cox with its fluted Corinthian columns.
© photographer Derry Moore

35. The drawing room at Castletown Cox with its ornate Rococo plasterwork frieze and Georgian fireplace. © photographer Derry Moore

36. A room with a view! The magnificent plasterwork door surrounds and pediments at Castletown Cox. © photographer Derry Moore

37. A formal dinner at Birr Castle from 'Stately Meals', a pilot TV programme filmed at the home of the 7th Earl of Rosse, August 1981. From left to right: Princess Harshad Puma Devi of Mori (back to camera); Brendan Parsons, 7th Earl of Rosse; Gareth de Brun; Ulli de Breffny (in front of window); Patrick, Lord Lichfield; Lady Alison Rosse; Desmond Fitzgerald, 29th Knight of Glyn; and Baron Brian de Breffny (back to camera).

38. Second screenshot from 'Stately Meals' showing side view of Ulli next to Lord Lichfield and Brian obscured by Princess Harshad Puma Devi of Mori.

39. An outdoor meal at Birr Castle from the pilot TV programme 'Stately Meals'. From left to right: Patrick, Lord Lichfield; Ulli de Breffny; Princess Harshad Puma Devi of Mori; Garech de Brun; Baron de Breffny (standing); Lady Alison Rosse (in background) and Patrick Parsons, Lord Oxmantown.

40. The Marriage of 7th Viscount Thomas de Vesci and Sita-Maria de Breffny, with Sita's father Brian in the background next to her mother Princess Jyotsna of Burdwan.

41. Abbeyleix House, the de Vesci family home, where Thomas and Sita lived for the first few years of their marriage, before it had to be sold to pay inheritance tax.

42. Sita, Viscountess de Vesci, and Thomas, Viscount de Vesci, at Ascot.

43. Ulli in the late 1980s just prior to Brian's death.

in 1990,[217] but was only sold in 1995 at the reduced price of almost £3 million to financier David Davies, who purchased the house and 1,300 acres of the land.[218]

Antiques and other collectibles were auctioned off including seventeenth, eighteenth and nineteenth century furniture, paintings, sculpture, oriental rugs and carpets, a rare private collection of antique pistols and guns and the contents of the family library. Viscount di Vesci said it was heart-breaking to see the house he grew up in sold and the furniture dispersed,[219] although they kept a cottage with 400 wooded acres of land as a holiday home.[220]

'What makes moving even harder is that we can only take a small number of the contents with us' said Thomas; 'we only have room in our cottage and a small house in London for a handful of things'.[221] Actually, they moved to a house on the borders of Chelsea and Fulham, close to Chelsea Football Club in London, and, to fit in all their possessions, they also extended their property to include the house next door.

They employed an interior designer to oversee the work. Two floors were knocked into one to create a library; the first floor was knocked into one huge space and the double drawing room split into two. The house contains antique and contemporary treasures from Ireland, Italy and India.[222] The move from Abbeyleix to Fulham was very stark for the de Vescis.

Interestingly these Fulham houses are within walking distance of the road where Brian's mother (Sita's grandmother) Marguerite had lived and gone to school in the 1900s.

Sita became a fashion designer, launching her first collection of beach wear in 2004, which included handmade kaftans and tunics. She then expanded into shoes and bags. Thomas runs a small horticultural business.

12. A charmed life of literature and the arts

Brian had a fixation with Ireland as he searched for an Irish heritage for himself. He was an accomplished genealogist and became a well-respected author, writing and publishing several books on Irish history and architecture during his time in Rome by the time he and Ulli bought Castletown Cox in 1978: 'Bibliography of Irish Family History' (published 1974); 'The Houses of Ireland' co-written with Rosemary ffoliott (1975) and dedicated to his daughter Sita-Maria; 'Churches and Abbeys of Ireland' (1976); 'The Irish World' also written and co-edited with Rosemary ffoliott (1976) and 'Castles of Ireland' (1977).

It is said that while researching for his book 'The Houses of Ireland' he would turn up at grand houses unannounced, just let himself in and wander round taking notes, although on one occasion the chatelaine of one of the houses threatened to shoot him if he did not leave![223]

Others of his books written and published around this time included: 'The Land of Ireland' (1979), 'Heritage of Ireland' (1980), 'Irish Family Names, Origins and Locations' (1982), 'In the Steps of St Patrick' (1982) and 'Ireland: A Cultural Encyclopaedia' which was prepared under his general editorship in 1983. These were all distinguished and serious, well researched pieces.

The one interesting exception to all these books on Ireland was 'The Synagogue', published in 1978. The Synagogue is an in-depth study of the history of the synagogue itself and the cultural development of the Jewish people - it was a throwback to part of his real heritage.

A review in the Jewish Chronicle said: 'it is difficult to believe that this scholarly and sympathetic book was written by a non-Jew'.[224] Whilst Brian was not strictly Jewish he did of course have a Jewish father and a Jewish heritage going back many hundreds of years, which in most areas of his life he seemed to want to hide completely. In the book, however, he made no claim to that Jewish heritage.

Most of Brian's books included photographs taken by his friend George Mott. Mott produced a few other books in his own right, most notably 'Foro Italico' a book of photographs of the 12ft tall, monumental, nude statues ordered by Mussolini for the Stadio dei Marmi and built for the never held 1944 Olympic Games. They were first seen by Mott in 1962 and photographed twenty years later. 'The Foro Italico sustains a guileless, perhaps unique, male eroticism which is at odds with the grandiloquent intentions of its planner and creators in Mussolini's fascist regime'.[225]

Brian also wrote 'My First Naked Lady', a work of fiction published in 1981, an odd and somewhat salacious tale about a young boy and his aunt[226] and, in complete contrast, a biography of Elizabeth Hayes, Mother M. Ignatius, founder of the Missionary Franciscan Sisters of the Immaculate Conception, entitled 'Unless the Seed Die'.

He was co-editor of 'The Irish Ancestor' with Rosemary ffolliot, a journal published twice yearly between 1969 and 1986 which brought together articles on Irish genealogy, biography and history, and which was also under the direction of Guy Strutt.[227]

Brian wrote many articles for the Irish Ancestor including new research into the heritage of Oscar Wilde. It is interesting to note that Brian debunked Wilde's mother's belief that she had Italian forebears, showing that this had no foundation in fact.[228] Brian seemed to be well versed in exposing false claims made by others.

In 1984 he co-founded with Ann Reihill the Irish Arts Review, a periodical published four times a year and a leading art and design publication, which continues to this day. In addition, he wrote an article for the Architectural Digest in 1983 about the refurbishment of Castletown Cox.

He was a keen supporter of the Wexford Opera Festival and the Irish Architectural Archive in Dublin,[229] and gave lectures on his areas of expertise. One such was at the Wexford Historical Society's Festival entitled 'The Truth and the Legend of St Patrick', reported in the local paper, with Brian called the 'well-known television and radio broadcaster'.[230]

Brian had, through these significant publications and appearances transformed himself into an accomplished author and fierce defender of Irish architecture and culture. He had created a persona which established him as kind and charming and was recognised as such by his friends, who overlooked his pretentions. However, those pretentions were not as harmless as some thought them to be.

13. A tangled web

Brian's life in Ireland may have made him seem charming and erudite to those that knew him there, but his convoluted tales about his early life led inexorably to complications: he had to distance himself from his parents, lie about his parentage and criminally falsify documents.

As far as is known his parents never visited him, or lived with him, in Ireland at Castletown Cox. There are no records of them after 1960 in Salt Lake City and they do not appear on any electoral registers in England in the next twenty years before their deaths; they may well have been living in an apartment in Malaga, Spain as this is the residential address given on Marguerite's death certificate.

Both, however, were in England at the time of their deaths. They died within weeks of each other; his mother, Marguerite, on 1st October 1980, and his father, Moses, on 4th January 1981 - perhaps as a consequence of his wife's death - and were in the adjoining counties of Bedfordshire and Hertfordshire, England, at the time.

Marguerite died in the Luton and Dunstable Hospital of bronchopneumonia and cerebral haemorrhage (stroke). Moses died 13 weeks later just 15 miles away in Fairfield Mental Hospital, Hitchin, suffering from bronchopneumonia and senile dementia. Both of these were NHS hospitals; not quite the expensive private clinic in Dublin that Brian spent his final weeks in a couple of years later.

Marguerite must have been staying in or around Luton so that she could be close to Moses who may well have come back to England to be treated for his senile dementia in Fairfield Hospital. However, it appears that they both developed bronchopneumonia, possibly due to the change in climate from the warmth of Malaga to the colder English winter and the higher circulation of viruses in the cold weather.

How much contact Brian had with his parents in the intervening years between their time in Salt Lake City and their deaths is not known. His daughter Sita never mentions them in the reminiscences of her life with Brian in Rome or Castletown Cox, and indeed said that 'he is not a man given to reminiscing about the past. I know next to nothing about his earlier years'.[231]

Did Brian have a falling out with his parents which led to him keeping them at arm's length, or was it just that they didn't fit into the life he had invented for himself? Whatever the reason was, he did have enough contact to be present to register their deaths, and what we do know for certain is that their death certificates are a tissue of lies.

Anyone registering a death must sign to certify that the particulars given are true to the best of their knowledge and belief. To wilfully give a false answer is a crime[232] but Brian seemed to have had no qualms about committing this criminal act and lying when registering their deaths.

To maintain the illusion of his Irish barony he had to distance himself from his real father and invent a fantasy father. So, his mother's death certificate states her occupation as 'wife of Maurice Leese, medical practitioner. Retired' and her usual address as Malaga, Spain. Brian certifies he is her son and that his name is Brian O'Rorke de Breffny[233] - a fabrication. Maurice (real name Moses) was never a medical practitioner, but this falsehood was necessary to fit in with Brian's other lies about his past. He also gets his mother's date of birth wrong: she was born in 1896 not 1894.

His father's death certification is even more of a fabrication, with the only correct pieces of information being his father's name - on this certificate down as Moses (not Maurice) Leese - and his date of birth (5th February 1900). Brian certified that Moses was born in the United States - not true, as we know he was born in the East End of London; that he was a medical practitioner (retired) - not true: as far as can be ascertained his only occupations in England were as a bookmaker and taxi driver. In Salt Lake City he worked in a bookshop and then as a travelling salesman. On the death certificate Brian puts his name down as 'Brian O'Rorke de Breffny', a repeat of the lie told on his mother's death certificate. He was plain old Brian Michael Leese; and worst of all he certified that he was his father Moses' stepson![234]

He signed himself 'Breffny' on both certificates in a shameless act, as if he were a real member of the aristocracy. To top it all the words 'normal signature' are written alongside it, presumably by the Registrar, on his father's death certificate.

The implication of these falsehoods is to suggest that his mother, Marguerite, was previously married to someone who passed on the O'Rorke de Breffny name and barony to Brian (because titles must pass down the male line), and that Moses, her only and real husband, was her second husband who became Brian's stepfather.

It is interesting in this regard to look back at Brian and Jyotsna's marriage certificate where he says his father is 'Maurice Michael Leese de Breffny and that his father's profession is Baron de Breffny of independent means'. So over the years he transformed his father Moses Leese, a Jewish East Ender by birth, into the Irish Baron de Breffny, and then into his American stepfather in an astounding work of pure fiction.

The family left behind in London

Did Moses, Marguerite and Brian have any contact with the Leese family back in London after their move to Utah? It's impossible to say. Moses' mother Rebecca died in 1957 at the age of eighty-three, in Finchley, London, and there is no evidence of Moses returning to England for her funeral. He left behind three sisters, Esther who lived into her nineties, Catherine into her eighties; and his young sister Dorothy who lived into her eighties until 1995. His brother Joseph died in his seventies and my grandfather, his brother Henry, died in 1965.

My mother died in 2003, and she often talked about her aunts Nancy

(Hannah) and Kitty (Catherine) and kept in touch with several of her cousins, but neither my mother nor anyone else in the family knew of Moses' and Marguerite's whereabouts or their deaths, and I am sure Brian would not have wanted them to, given the lies on their death certificates.

Brian's death notice in the press listed many of the great and the good from his family and friends around the world who were in attendance at his death and funeral and ended with 'his cousins'.[235] It is unclear which 'cousins' were being talked about here. Certainly not my mother.

He cut himself off completely, not wanting to talk about or remember his earlier life, and his daughter Sita's rather ironic words ring hollow: 'He had always remained consistent not only to his beliefs and values but also in his tremendous loyalty to his friends and family'.[236]

QBDAC 280672

CERTIFIED COPY   **OF AN ENTRY**

DEATH	Entry No.	88

Registration district *Luton*

Sub-district *Luton*   Administrative area *County of Bedfordshire.*

1. Date and place of death *First October 1980.*
Luton and Dunstable Hospital, Luton

2. Name and surname *Marguerite Mary LEESE.*

3. Sex *Female.*

4. Maiden surname of woman who has married *ODELL.*

5. Date and place of birth *6. January 1894. London.*

6. Occupation and usual address *Wife of Maurice LEESE. Medical Practitioner. Retired Alegranza 31 - E. Benalmadena Costa Malaga. SPAIN.*

7.(a) Name and surname of informant *Brian O'Rorke de BREFFNY*

(b) Qualification *Son.*

(c) Usual address *Castletown House, Carrick-on-Suir, Co. Tipperary. EIRE.*

8. Cause of death
1 a. Bronchopneumonia.
b. Cerebral Haemorrhage.

Certified by Carol Blow. MB.

9. I certify that the particulars given by me above are true to the best of my knowledge and belief .... *B. Breffny* .... Signature of informant

10. Date of registration *Second October 1980.*

11. Signature of registrar *S. J. Kenny Registrar*

CERTIFIED to be a true copy of an entry in the certified copy of* a register of Births, Still-births or Deaths in the District above mentioned. Given at the GENERAL REGISTER OFFICE, under the Seal of the said Office on   28th   July   2021
*If the Certificate is given from the original Register, the words "the certified copy of" are struck out.

CAUTION: THERE ARE OFFENCES RELATING TO FALSIFYING OR ALTERING A CERTIFICATE AND USING OR POSSESSING A FALSE CERTIFICATE. © CROWN COPYRIGHT

WARNING: A CERTIFICATE IS NOT EVIDENCE OF IDENTITY.
2031847 04/21 AFS/A35P

CHE

44. © Crown Copyright. Brian's mother's Death Certificate with an incorrect year of birth and showing her as the wife of Maurice Leese, a retired medical practitioner, when his name was Moses Leese, and there is no evidence that he was a medical practitioner.

Application Number11952345/1

QBDAC 246441

CERTIFIED COPY OF AN ENTRY

| DEATH | Entry No. | 1.14 |

| Registration district | BIGGLESWADE | Administrative area County of Bedfordshire |
| Sub-district | BIGGLESWADE | |

1. Date and place of death

Fourth January 1981

Fairfield Hospital Stotfold

2. Name and surname

Moses LEESE

3. Sex *Male*

4. Maiden surname of woman who has married —

5. Date and place of birth

5th February 1900

United States

6. Occupation and usual address

Medical Practitioner (Retired)

Fairfield Hospital Stotfold Hitchin Herts

7. (a) Name and surname of informant

Brian O'Rorke de BREFFNY

(b) Qualification *Step-son*

(c) Usual address

Castletown Carrick na Suir Tipperary Eire

8. Cause of death

I (a) Bronchopneumonia.

II Senile Dementia.

Certified by L.C. De Silva M.B.

9. I certify that the particulars given by me above are true to the best of my knowledge and belief. *Breffny* ████████ Signature of informant

10. Date of registration

Fifth January 1981

11. Signature of registrar

A Christopher Interim Registrar

45. © Crown Copyright. Brian's father's Death Certificate with his name now correct as Moses Leese and correct date of birth, but showing his place of birth as the United States when it was Stoney Lane, Aldgate, in the East End of London; there is no evidence he was a medical practitioner, and Brian was certainly NOT his stepson!

76

14. Written in stone

Brian died of prostate cancer and renal failure on 11th February 1989 at his home, Castletown Cox. He had spent many weeks in the newly built, private, Blackrock Clinic in Dublin, having major surgery there in November 1988,[237] and was then nursed at home for his final days before slipping into a coma just before he died.

What is surprising is that it was one of Ulli's daughters, Lena, who registered his death,[238] classifying herself as his daughter. Lena, born Lena Agneta Lillas, was Lena Solomon at the time of Brian's death, and Lena Scurfield at the time of her mother's death. She, along with her three sisters, had been adopted by Sir Stafford Sands when Ulli was married to him. It is not known if Brian also formally adopted them, or if they just called themselves his daughters.

His death certificate records his name as Brian de Breffny and his age as sixty, but as we know he was originally Brian Michael Leese aged just fifty-eight. These errors are perhaps unsurprising as Lena, given she was not a direct relative, might not have known his correct details - and perhaps that was the reason she was sent to register the death, although there is no evidence that his family were involved in the deceptions, or were aware of them.

There was a funeral mass held for him followed by his burial in Whitechurch graveyard beside Castletown Cox[239] and in that graveyard there is a headstone which bears the most remarkable inscription: 'Brian de Breffny 1929 - 1989 born Cimiez, Alpes-Maritimes, France, died Castletown Cox County Kilkenny'. So Brian's fabrications about his life ended up not only on his death certificate and his parents death certificates, but also followed him to the grave, written in stone.

He left an estate of £421,694.00 (£1.2 million at 2021 values).[240] However, when Castletown Cox and its contents were sold in 1991 far greater sums were realised.

His wife Ulli was apparently heart-broken by his death, and many friends and family eulogised him, but Auberon Waugh in an 'unkind obituary in the Daily Telegraph' described him, not without some merit, as a 'conman and a pretentious snob' who lived a lie[241] and scathingly called him 'Count de Cabbie'.

46. Gravestone in Whitechurch Cemetery, Ireland, with Brian's assumed name Brian de Breffny, with an incorrect year of birth (it was 1931) and incorrect place of birth (he was not born in France but in Twickenham, London).

15. Why did he do it?

What was Brian's motivation for all the deception and falsehood that littered his life? Perhaps he started out with a plan to radically change his life; to meet (and marry) people who could advance his status and situation; or perhaps he just drifted into it, taking opportunities as they arose.

Did he suffer from a condition such as Pseudologia Fantastica (pathological lying) where people create stories to impress others, often assuming important roles? Questions and doubts expressed by others lead patients with this condition to further elaboration to satisfy the listener, and new lies are needed to cover the old ones.[242]

As time went by it may have been that the deception and lies became impossible to extricate himself from, and obfuscation was the easier option. Maybe he wanted to leave the past behind and forget about it altogether for some reason. Perhaps he enjoyed the process of deception.

It can't have been easy trying to keep up the pretences he had invented for himself. Maybe he just didn't care. Many national newspapers at the time of his death found it hard to get the facts right about him, with the Irish Independent describing him as 'a native of Paris who came to reside at Castletown'[243] and The Times in their obituary saying that he was born in Paris, and educated there at the Sorbonne (one of the stories he told while he was in Rome and which is reiterated on his gravestone, which gives his place of birth as the south of France), but the Daily Telegraph, more accurately, had his correct place of birth and parentage.[244]

Had he got what he wanted? It would appear so. He ended up with a rich and beautiful wife, and a luxury lifestyle in a Palladian Mansion, and was once voted Ireland's best dressed man. He must have been delighted when his daughter married into the British aristocracy with close connections to the Royal Family.

Did Brian ever change his name legally? This is unclear; but he changed his name several times in his life: Brian Michael Leese - Brian Lees - Brian de Breffny - Brian Michael Leese de Breffny - Baron de Breffny - Brian O'Rourke de Breffny - Baron O'Rorke de Breffny - Count O'Rourke - and even '7th Baron of the Holy Roman Empire' according to Auberon Waugh in an obituary in the Sunday Telegraph.

Many Jews and people with Jewish forebears anglicised their names, or distanced themselves from their heritage, because of the antisemitism that dogged their lives. Brian however went much further than this, creating a whole new persona for himself, and his deception went far beyond changing his name. He put false information about his father on his first marriage certificate and on his father's death certificate, calling Moses his stepfather.

Was he happy? We have to assume he was. He had achieved an amazing transformation from taxi driver's son to wealthy 'baron' in one short lifetime.

A complex character and inveterate liar, Brian was also an intelligent and erudite man. He had acquired for himself extensive genealogical and architectural knowledge. He had literary talent, writing numerous books on Irish history and architecture and even a novel. He edited, researched and wrote for architectural and arts periodicals. He seems to have been genuinely liked and loved.

Would I have liked him if I had met him? Maybe I would, for all of it. He was my mother's cousin and my first cousin once removed.

References

1. Two lucky escapes

[1] Jarrett Ross Sephardic Genealogy blogspot 2016

[2] Marriage certificate 1965 no.68 Gt Synagogue Chambers Morris Liest and Hannah Dickie

[3] Colour coded Map of Jewish East London 1899.

[4] Both Moses and Hannah were illiterate and signed their marriage certificate with their marks.

[5] Census and birth certificate spellings of the family surname include Leis, Leese, Lease and then Lees. Some of these changes may have been due to Morris being illiterate (Myer and Fanny's birth certificates just have his mark); others may have been due to people writing the name phonetically and some may be due to Anglicisation of the family name.

[6] Birth certificate 1874 no.363 Myer Lees

[7] 1881 Census

[8] Marriage certificate 1892 no.4 East London Synagogue. Myer Leese and Rebecca Joseph

[9] London School Board records and 1901 Census

[10] A Look Back at Life in London's East End, Ian McPherson, 1st May 2018, City Matters, City Publishing Ltd.

[11] 1901 census

[12] Birth certificate 1900 no.95 Moses Leese

[13] London School Board records. Esther started school on 3rd July 1899 and Moses on 9th February 1903; both were aged three at

the time they started. In Victorian times many children started school at the age of three or four, sometimes for the reason that there was no-one at home to care for them as their parents had to work. They then left school themselves at a very early age to go out to work on their own account.

[14] 1911 Census

[15] School Admissions and Discharges, 1840-1911

[16] 1911 Census

2. The Leese family in the thirties

[17] Joyce Lees was my mother, the daughter of Henry, Moses' younger brother

[18] Henry Lees birth certificate

[19] 1911 Census

[20] Marriage certificate 1923 no.132 Maurice (Moses) Lees and Marguerite O'Dell

[21] Thomas Henry Dey was himself the subject of indictment at the Old Bailey charged with keeping a gaming house within the meaning of the 'Betting House Act' although this indictment was not presented in court.

[22] 1921 Census

[23] Crime and Investigation.co.uk

[24] 'Peaky Blinders: The Legacy' by Carl Chinn, publisher John Blake

[25] 1921 Census

[26] Ibid.

[27] Birmingham Mail, 28th November 2013 'The Real Peaky Blinders' by Carl Chinn

[28] Crime and Investigation.co.uk

[29] A number of first names changed in the family: Myer became Michael / Mickey; Moses became Morris / Maurice / Mickey junior, Hannah was known as Nancy and Catherine was also called Kate and Kitty: Joyce Lees (Brian's cousin) knew them as Aunt Nancy and Aunt Kitty.

[30] 1922 London Telephone Directory

[31] Marriage certificate 1923 no.132 Maurice (Moses) Lees and Marguerite O'Dell

[32] Birth certificate no. 26 Marguerite Mary O'Dell born 6th January 1896 at 1 Marlborough Street, Chelsea North

[33] School Admissions registers – Marguerite was admitted to Langford Road School in August 1899 aged two and a half but was removed just five months later in January 1900 as being 'too delicate'. She was then readmitted in July of the same year. School Admissions and Discharges, 1840-1911

[34] School Board for London, Hammersmith and Fulham, Langford School Admission and Discharge Register for Infants

[35] 1930 Telephone Directory and 1930 Electoral Register

[36] 1934 Electoral Register, 1936 Telephone Directory

[37] There are some accounts of Moses and Marguerite having a child called Antoinette who was born and died on 10th May 1925, but no corroborating evidence (i.e. birth or death certificates) can be found for this.

[38] Brian Michael Leese birth certificate.

[39] 1934 Richmond upon Thames Electoral Roll

[40] My grandfather (Moses' brother Henry), grandmother Rose and my mother Joyce lived in Cornwall Road and then Sidney Road between 1932 and 1935; his brother Joe lived in Winchester Road and then Sidney Road from 1930 to 1939; his sister Esther and family lived in St Margaret's Road; his sister Nancy and family lived in St Margaret's Road and then at 66 Gordon Road after Moses moved to St Margaret's Road. These locations are all within a few streets of each other in Twickenham

[41] There could be more cousins, but these are the only ones I have been able to trace.

[42] Sunday Tribune (Dublin) 8th January 1989 Chairs and Graces article by Sita de Breffny

3. The war years

[43] 1939 Census and Electoral Register

[44] Royal Airforce Airman records 1918-1940

[45] London Vintage Taxi Association, London Taxi History.

[46] Angus Calder, The People's War, Panther Books 1971, p43
[47] Brian's birth certificate and Moses marriage certificate
[48] RMS Queen Elizabeth Passenger List 1949
[49] United States immigration service Declaration of Intention 13171
[50] RMS Queen Elizabeth Passenger list 1950

4. A new life in Salt Lake City

[51] 24th May 1950 Deseret News SLC Utah
[52] Ibid
[53] 7th June 1950 Deseret News SLC Utah
[54] 27th September 1950 Deseret News SLC Utah
[55] 4th August 1950 Deseret News and 29th September 1951 The North Ogden News
[56] 8th October and then 25th November 1950 the Ogden (Utah) Standard-Examiner
[57] RMS Mauretania passenger list 1953
[58] 28th August 1953 Deseret News
[59] 21st November 1953 Deseret News
[60] 23rd January 1954 Deseret News
[61] 11th June 1954; The Daily Herald, 8th January 1955; Deseret News, 12th February 1955; Ogden Standard-Examiner, 24th March 1955; The Times News, Nephi, Utah; and 11th June 1955 Deseret News
[62] Salt Lake City Directories 1951, 1952, 1953, 1957,1959, 1960
[63] ZCMI was a Mormon enterprise set up in 1868 by Brigham Young who also founded Salt Lake City and who was the second president of the Church of Latter-day Saints.
[64] Utah Pharmacy Digest, January 1957
[65] 11th February 1951 Deseret News p.17
[66] 12th November 1950 Deseret News p.49
[67] 30th November 1950 Deseret News p.24
[68] 13th December 1953 Salt Lake Tribune p66
[69] 6th March 1955 Ogden Standard Examiner
[70] 6th January 1960 The Herald Journal, Logan, Utah.
[71] 10th and 11th August 1969 The Herald Journal.

[72] Pan American World Airlines Passenger Manifest 1st June 1956

[73] Geneva features later in this story as Brian said he had a 'godmother' living there and went there himself on at least one occasion.

[74] Swissair Passenger Manifest 15th June 1956

[75] 1953 passage on the RMS Mauretania from Cobh, Ireland

5. The O'Rourke barony

[76] Dictionary of Pseudonyms p137, Adrian Room 5th edition. McFarland and co. 2014

[77] Bibliography of Irish Family History and Genealogy, Brian de Breffny, Golden Eagle Books, Cork 1973 ISBN 0 85342 398 9

[78] The kingdom comprised approximately the area of the Roman Catholic Diocese of Kilmore

[79] The Case of the O'Rourke, Prince of Breifne, posted on Reddit inc. Irish Chiefs 2021

[80] IrishIdentity.com 'Cromwell's Bloody Campaign'

[81] O'Rourke Family Genealogy and History, The O'Ruairc History Index rootsweb.com

[82] Emily Hourican, the Irish Independent 'Tale of a Baron's Court' 2nd October 2011

6. The celebrity playground of Ischia

[83] A History of Ischia, Dion Protani, Ischia Review, ischiareview.com

[84] William Walton 'Behind the Façade' by Susana Walton, Oxford University Press 1988 p38

[85] Ibid. p116

[86] Sunday Independent 10th April 1988 p12

[87] William Walton 'Behind the Façade' by Susana Walton, Oxford University Press 1988 p112

[88] Ibid. p114

[89] Ibid. p185

[90] Sunday Independent 10th April 1988 p12

[91] Brian de Breffny by Ciaran MacGonical, Dictionary of Irish Biography October 2009

[92] Emily Hourican, the Independent 'The Tale of a Baron's Court' 2nd October 2011

[93] Flight Glasgow to New York 3rd December 1959 and Mexico City to New York 4th February 1960 shows Casa Montevergine as Brian's permanent address

[94] Emily Hourican, the Independent 'The Tale of a Baron's Court' 2nd October 2011

[95] Martin Stannard 'Muriel Spark The Biography' p.432 Weidenfeld and Nicolson 2009

[96] Martin Stannard interview with George Mott 4th May 1994 referenced in his biography of Muriel Spark p385 Weidenfeld and Nicolson 2009

[97] 6th January 1960 The Herald Journal, Logan, Utah

[98] 7th January 1960 The Leader, Garland Times Utah

[99] Air France Flights Glasgow to New York 3rd December 1959 and Mexico City to New York 4th February 1960

[100] Emily Hourican, the Independent 'Tale of a Baron's Court' 2nd October 2011

7. A secret marriage to an Indian princess

[101] Birmingham Post 30th September 1960

[102] Ibid.

[103] Knight Commander of the Order of the Indian Empire

[104] The Zamindari System was introduced by Lord Cornwallis in 1793 through the Permanent Settlement Act giving Zamindars (hereditary landowners) the right to collect rent from the farmers who became tenants. The tax was to be paid even at times of poor harvests.

[105] Evening Standard 29th September 1960

[106] Marriage Certificate no. 26 Bridgnorth, Shropshire 24th September 1960

[107] At this point Brian's father Moses was still in Salt Lake City working as a travelling salesman for the Mormons

[108] Birth notice, West London Star Group 13th July 1962

[109] Emily Hourican, the Independent 'Tale of a Baron's Court' 2nd October 2011

[110] Sunday Independent (Dublin) 9th September 1990

[111] Birth Certificate Sita-Maria Arabella de Breffny, St Marylebone, 6th July 1962

[112] Irish Independent Weekend 1st August 2009

[113] Evening Standard 10th December 1965 and Birmingham Post 11th December 1965

[114] 23rd July 1968 The Aberdeen Press and Journal

[115] 23rd July 1968 The Bangor Daily News, Maine p22

[116] 'The Men Who Stare at Hens' by Simon Leyland, The History Press Ireland, 2019

8. The glamour of life in Rome

[117] Sunday Tribune (Dublin) article by Sita-Maria de Breffny 8th January 1989

[118] Martin Stannard interview with Guy Strutt 15th January 2001 quoted in his biography of Muriel Spark

[119] Sunday Tribune article by Sita-Maria de Breffny 8th January 1989

[120] Irish Independent Weekend 1st August 2009

[121] Brian de Breffny by Ciaran MacGonigal, Dictionary of Irish Biography October 2009

[122] Usual translation 'The sweet life'

[123] Guardian 28th April 2014

[124] 9th April 1966 Deseret News

[125] 14th May 1966 Deseret News

[126] 9th April 1966 Deseret News

[127] 'The Little Family go to America 'an article on SCRIBD, a digital platform for books and other material posted by Mike Standish

[128] 10th and 11th August 1969 The Herald Journal, Logan, Utah

[129] Martin Stannard biography of Muriel Spark Weidenfeld and Nicolson 2009

[130] Brian met Muriel Spark in Rome in about 1970 and they became close friends.

[131] Martin Stannard biography of Muriel Spark p. 432 Weidenfeld and Nicolson 2009

[132] Zion's Co-operative Mercantile Institution

[133] SLC Directory 1952 and RMS Mauretania passenger list 6th July 1953

[134] 'The Synagogue', Brian de Breffny, Macmillan 1978

[135] Ibid.

[136] The Herald Statesman, New York 13th October 1977

[137] Martin Stannard interview with Guy Strutt 15th January 2001 quoted in his biography of Muriel Spark

[138] National Library of Scotland, Muriel Spark in Rome

[139] 17th April 2006 Obituary in The Guardian

[140] Queen Frederica was at this time living in exile in Rome having had to leave Greece following the 1967 coup

[141] Martin Stannard biography of Muriel Spark p. 419 Weidenfeld and Nicolson 2009

[142] Sunday Tribune (Ireland) article 'Chairs and Graces' by Sita de Breffny 8th January 1989

[143] 5th July 2014 Susanna Rustin interview with Penelope Jardine in The Guardian

[144] 15th September 2010 The Atlantic magazine, Washington DC

[145] Martin Stannard interview with Dario Ambrosiani 18th November 1994 quoted in his biography of Muriel Spark p. 384

[146] Martin Stannard biography of Muriel Spark p. 430 Weidenfeld and Nicolson 2009

[147] Ibid. p. 442

[148] Martin Stannard interview with George Mott 4th May 1994, quoted in his biography of Muriel Spark

[149] Martin Stannard biography of Muriel Spark p. 429 Weidenfeld and Nicolson 2009

9. A Finnish heiress, the Nazis and the Mafia

[150] Emily Hourican, the Independent 'Tale of a Baron's Court' 2nd October 2011

[151] Life Magazine 3rd February 1967 'Scandal in the Bahamas' p. 62/63

[152] The Tribune, Nassau Bahamas. Kevin Evans, 'Dynamic Duo of Politicians', 7th January 2019

[153] Sir Randol Fawkes, leader of the Labour Party, won a Parliamentary seat in the 1967 election that brought about majority Black rule in the Bahamas

[154] 'The Faith that Moved the Mountain', Sir Randol Fawkes 1979

[155] 15th July 1951, The Boston Globe

[156] 21st October 1961, The Pittsburgh Courier

[157] 20th October 1961, Evening Standard London

[158] 25th February 1962, The Honolulu Advertiser

[159] 'The Sink – Terror, Crime and Dirty Money in the Offshore World' by Jeffrey Robinson, Constable 2003

[160] In 1939 the Bahamian House of Assembly, including Sands, amended the Lotteries and Gaming Act (1927) to allow the Governor in Council to grant annual Certificates of Exemption to allow gaming for two clubs with a number of restrictions.

[161] 'Bahamian Fragments', Jim W Baker

[162] Germany's ability to produce and deploy weapons such as submarines, battleships and an expanded Army were all limited by the Versailles Treaty.

[163] Claus von Stauffenberg and other conspirators attempted to assassinate Hitler, inside his Wolf's Lair field headquarters near Rastenburg, East Prussia. The name Operation Valkyrie—originally referring to part of the conspiracy—has become associated with the entire event.

[164] 17th July 1962, The Nassau Daily Tribune

[165] 8th September 1962, The Nassau Daily Tribune

[166] Otto Skorzeny was a prominent SS officer tasked with special missions by Hitler, notably the freeing of Mussolini from an Italian prison in 1943, when troops commanded by Skorzeny landed by glider on the roof of the prison in a surprise attack and overwhelmed the guards. He never denounced Nazism and in 1958 purchased Martinstown House, a large estate in County Kildare, Ireland.

[167] 8th September 1962, The Nassau Daily Tribune

[168] 'The Sink – Terror, Crime and Dirty Money in the Offshore World' by Jeffrey Robinson, Constable 2003

[169] Bahamian Fragments, Jim W Baker

[170] 'The Sink – Terror, Crime and Dirty Money in the Offshore World' by Jeffrey Robinson, Constable 2003

[171] Encyclopaedia Britannica, Britannica.com 11th January 2022

[172] 'The Secret Life of J Edgar Hoover' by Anthony Summers, Open Road Media 2013

173 New Bahamas Prime Minister Lynden Pindling asked Queen
Elizabeth II to set up the Royal Commission to look into the
questionable fees accepted by former Government Ministers and
Crime syndicate members running the casinos

174 The Miami Herald, 22nd August 1967 p.14

175 Time magazine. 'The Bahamas: Consultant's Paradise Lost' 8th
September 1967

176 Bahamianology.com

177 Villacorner.com

178 Los Angeles Times, 14th February 1988

179 The Miami Herald, 30th January 1966 p.130

180 Ibid.

181 The Palm Beach Post, 24th August 1967, p10.

182 Ibid.

183 'The Tale of a Baron's Court', Emily Hourican, the Independent
2nd October 2011

184 Tribune article 'Chairs and Graces' by Sita de Breffny 8th January
1989

185 Sunday Independent (Dublin) 25th December 1988

10. A lavish life in a Palladian mansion

186 Aristocratic titles are not officially recognised in the Republic
of Ireland and the role of the College of Arms in interpreting
eligibility in cases of dispute is also not recognised, so Brian was
able to adopt this title with ease, particularly as he had already
been using the surname 'de Breffny' and the title 'Baron' for some
time. Many people were sceptical about his title but they appear
to have been prepared to keep quiet so that they could go to Castletown Cox and enjoy the largesse of their hosts.

187 William Walton 'Behind the Façade' by Susana Walton, Oxford
University Press 1988 p. 226

188 Ibid. p. 233 -234

189 Ibid. p. 236

190 Ibid. Acknowledgements

191 Emily Hourican, the Independent, 'The Tale of a Baron's Court'
2nd October 2011

[192] Irish Independent News, Independent.ie 25th November 2018

[193] Sunday Independent (Dublin) 9th September 1990

[194] Emily Hourican, the Independent 'Tale of a Baron's Court' 2nd October 2011

[195] Letter from Brian de Breffny, Sunday Independent (Dublin) 20th November 1988

[196] The Architectural Digest, 'Magnificent Obsession' by Brian de Breffny August 1983

[197] Ibid.

[198] The Irish Revolutionary Period (1910s to early 1920s) when Irish nationalist opinion shifted its gravity from the Irish Parliamentary Party which supported Home Rule within the British state and which allowed its MPs to sit in the UK House of Commons, to republican Sinn Fein which advocated an independent Ireland with its own legislative system.

[199] Irish Republican Army

[200] Desmond Fitzgerald was the 29th and last Knight of Glin.

[201] 'The Houses of Ireland' Brian de Breffny and Rosemary ffolliot, Viking Press 1975 p.143

[202] 'In the Houses of Ireland' by Marianne Heron, Stewart, Tabori & Chang Inc. 1988

[203] Irish Independent review 4th October 1986

[204] Irish Independent 19th October 1991

[205] Irish Independent 8th October 1991

[206] Irish Independent News, Independent.ie 25th November 2018

11. Sita-Maria and a royal connection

[207] From 1960 to 1978 Lord Snowdon was married to Princess Margaret, the younger sister of Queen Elizabeth II.

[208] Sunday Independent 30th April 1995

[209] Belfast Telegraph 8th January 1965

[210] Belfast Telegraph 5th January 1965

[211] Sunday Independent 21st June 1987

[212] Sunday World (Dublin) 6th September 1987

[213] Irish Independent 22nd August 1987

[214] Irish Independent 7th September 1987 p6

215 Irish Independent 30th January 1998, classified advertisements section

216 Irish Independent 19th May 1990

217 Irish Independent 10th May 1990

218 Irish Independent 6th January 1995

219 Evening Herald 25th April 1995

220 Sunday Tribune 30th April 1995

221 Sunday Independent 23rd April 1995

222 Irish Independent Weekend 1st August 2009

12. A charmed life of literature and the arts

223 'The Men Who Stare at Hens' Simon Leyland, The History Press Ireland, 2019

224 Meir Persoff, The Jewish Chronicle 29th September 1978

225 'Foro Italico', Powerhouse Books, New York 2003 with an editorial by Georgio Armani

226 The Observer 6th September 1981 Book Review

227 Foreword to 'Pedigrees of Some of Emperor Charlemagne's Descendants' volume II Genealogical Publishing Company 2009

228 Canberra Times 13th August 1994 Review of 'Mother of Oscar' by Joy Melville

229 Brian de Breffny by Ciaran MacGonigal, Dictionary of Irish Biography October 2009

230 New Ross Standard, Ireland, 2nd November 1984

13. A tangled web

231 Sunday Tribune 8th January 1989 'Chairs and Graces' article by Sita de Breffny

232 Perjury Act 1911 Chapter 6, False Statements as to Births and Deaths, maximum penalty two years imprisonment or a fine, or both.

233 Marguerite Leese death certificate Luton, Bedfordshire entry 88

234 Moses Leese death certificate Biggleswade, Bedfordshire entry 144

235 13th February 1989 Irish Independent

236 Sunday Tribune article 'Chairs and Graces' by Sita de Breffny 8th Jan 1989

14. Written in stone

[237] Sunday Independent (Dublin) 27th November 1988

[238] Brian de Breffny death certificate issued in Ireland, registration no. 1001577 16th February 1989

[239] Irish Independent 13th February 1989

[240] Sunday Tribune 14th January 1990

[241] 'Tale of a Baron's Court', Emily Hourican, the Independent 2nd October 2011

[242] 'Pseudologia Fantastica', Author Petra Garlipp, Oxford Clinical Psychiatry 2017 p319

[243] Irish Independent 13th February 1989

[244] Sunday Independent (Dublin) 5th March 1989